HOW TO CUT YOUR MORTGAGE IN HALF

Homeowner's Guide to Mortgages, Interest and Taxes

Vijay Fadia

IMPORTANT

Although care has been taken to ensure the accuracy and utility of the information and forms contained in this Manual, neither the publisher nor the author assumes any liability in connection with any use thereof. This publication is sold with the understanding that the publisher is not engaged in rendering legal, accounting, or other professional service. This book should not be used as a substitute for professional assistance essential to planning your finances. Consult a competent professional for answers to your specific questions.

Printed in the United States of America

Published by
HOMESTEAD PUBLISHING COMPANY

Table of Contents

Introduction to Cutting Your Mortgage in Half

1

Home ownership is an eternal American dream. From the time a person starts working his first job, his goal is to save enough money so he can make a down payment on a home of his dream. For this he would work overtime and weekends; he may even hold down a second job. He would skimp on the common luxuries or forgo vacations that he would otherwise be tempted to take. He may enroll in an automatic payroll deduction plan as part of a forced savings program. He and, if married, his wife will pool their resources together and set aside a certain sum every month that is earmarked for home ownership. They may even postpone having any children till such day as they are able to own their own home.

Eventually, if they have been working diligently toward their dream, one day they'll have sufficient money to take that magical step toward becoming proud owners of a home. They will scour every neighborhood looking for that dream house. In the tow of a real estate broker, they'll look at scores of houses until they come upon one that foots all the characteristics they had in mind: number of bedrooms, backyard, neighborhood, layout, and the right price.

Finding a Mortgage

Finding the right home was just the beginning. Now they have to find a lender (a savings and loan association or a bank or a mortgage broker) for the mortgage on the home. There will be loan applications to fill out, credit checks to be made, employments to be verified.

They will have to find their way through a bewildering array of mortgages and payment plans. There will be interest rates and monthly payments and prepayment penalties to contend with. The interest rate may be fixed or adjustable, the loan may or may not have negative amortization feature and the lender may require an impound account to pay insurance and taxes.

Their lender or the real estate broker may be of some help to them in sorting out all these confusing choices and guide them in making the right decisions. But then again, they may not get the right information or advice and may be left to fend for themselves.

If things have gone the way they should, one day the escrow on their dream house will close and they'll join the ranks of millions of other homeowners. Within a few short days they'll receive from their lender a book of payment coupons indicating the monthly mortgage they will be sending in each month. As is true in a vast majority of cases, they'll make regular monthly payments for the next thirty years before they own their home free and clear.

This is the scenario played out every day in every town in America. What's wrong with this scenario? Is there a missing piece of vital information in this puzzle? You bet.

Mortgage Trap

Not once throughout this process has anyone told the aspiring homeowner that he has just committed himself to paying back more than twice, even three times, the amount of the mortgage over thirty years. If he has borrowed $75,000 at 10% interest over 30 years, he'll be paying back almost $237,000. That's nearly $162,000 in interest charges - more than twice the amount borrowed. If he had financed $100,000 over 30 years at 13%, his interest expense on the loan would be $298,200, nearly three times the amount borrowed.

If someone had informed our new homeowner of the true amounts he would be paying back before he owns the home free and clear, he would simply be dumbfounded. During the first year of his ownership more than 98% of his monthly payments would go toward servicing the loan. In other words, less than 2% of the amounts paid would reduce the principal of the loan.

Way out of the Trap

But things do not have to be this way. You do not have to lock yourself in a thirty-year mortgage and pay hundreds of thousands of dollars in interest expense to own your home. By understanding how mortgages work, you'll be able to use little-known techniques to lighten the onerous burden of homeownership.

You'll be able to cut your standard 30-year mortgage by as much as 20, even 25, years. You'll be able to own your home while you're still in your prime income-producing years. Having paid off the mortgage sooner, you'll be freed of the constant worry of having to come up with a mortgage payment every month.

In fact, you'll have substantial extra cash on hand that you'll be able to put to use for your enjoyment. You'll have money for little luxuries, enjoy ski vacations, buy extra clothes, save money for the education of your children - things that other homeowners can't afford because they are still making regular monthly mortgage payments. You'll have realized your American dream in its truest sense.

Cut Interest Cost of All Borrowings

We briefly looked at the astounding cost of owning a home in terms of interest paid. Incidentally, throughout this book we use home mortgages to illustrate various points we are making regarding the cost of borrowing. But the same principles apply to other kinds of borrowings, such as auto loans, student loans, home improvement loans, so-called bill consolidation loans. We've targeted our discussion toward mortgages simply because it almost always represents the largest borrowing ever done by an individual and, therefore, represents the largest sum laid out as interest expense.

By using the principles taught in this book to cut down the cost of a home mortgage, you'll have achieved the greatest savings. As you begin to understand and apply these principles, you'll see potential savings in other areas too.

Interest Cost on a Loan

In order to give you an idea of how much you're paying in interest on your mortgage loan, we have prepared an Interest Factors table below. This table is designed for a 30-year, fixed-rate mortgage. The interest factors allow you to compute your total interest charges to be paid out over the term of the loan. You do this by simply multiplying the amount borrowed with the interest factor associated with your mortgage interest rate. If your interest rate falls between the rates listed here, you can use straight-line interpolation to approximate the applicable interest factor.

Interest Factors

7% = 1.395	10.5 = 2.293	14 = 3.266
7.25 = 1.456	10.75 = 2.361	14.25 = 3.337
7.5 = 1.517	11 = 2.428	14.5 = 3.408
7.75 = 1.579	11.25 = 2.497	14.75 = 3.480
8 = 1.642	11.5 = 2.565	15 = 3.552
8.25 = 1.705	11.75 = 2.634	15.25 = 3.624
8.5 = 1.768	12 = 2.703	15.5 = 3.696
8.75 = 1.832	12.25 = 2.772	15.75 = 3.769
9 = 1.897	12.5 = 2.842	16 = 3.841
9.25 = 1.962	12.75 = 2.912	16.25 = 3.914
9.5 = 2.027	13 = 2.982	16.5 = 3.987
9.75 = 2.093	13.25 = 3.053	16.75 = 4.059
10 = 2.159	13.5 = 3.124	17 = 4.132
10.25 = 2.226	13.75 = 3.194	17.25 = 4.206

$ _____   X_____ = $ _____
amount   interest   total interest
financed   factor   paid

$ _____   X_____ = $ _____
total interest   amount   total cost of
paid   financed   your mortgage

Here are the formulas you can use:

($ amount financed) X (interest factor) = $ total interest paid

($ total interest paid) + ($ amount borrowed) = $ total cost of your loan

Illustration: You're buying a home worth $150,000 by putting 10% as down payment, borrowing the rest (i.e., $135,000) at 10% fixed interest over 30 years. Using the interest factor from the table for 10%, you can determine that you'll pay $135,000 times 2.159 or $291,465 in total interest cost over the life of the mortgage. By adding this interest cost to the amount borrowed, you can determine that you'll pay $426,465 as the total cost of your mortgage.

Can You Afford This Mortgage?

2

You have been looking for your dream house for months. Finally, you find something that just catches your fancy. It has three bedrooms with two baths, just as you wanted. It has the right kind of carpeting and drapes that match your furniture. It is in the right location. The school for your child is only three blocks away. The house has "curb appeal" as the real estate agent pointed out to you the first time she drove you over.

But can you afford to buy this house?

This is the critical question that every home buyer asks himself in pursuit of his dream house. Each lender has his own lending policies and formulas that he uses to determine the qualifications of a potential buyer. But they all have certain basic criteria and, by learning about them and applying these standards to your own situation, you'll save yourself a great deal of time and heartache. After all, there is no point in looking at real estate if you cannot afford to buy it.

In this chapter, we'll look at these criteria to help you understand the lending process.

Lending Criteria

In general, there are three basic criteria that every lender uses:

1. **Down payment**

2. **Your credit history**

3. **Your ability to repay**

Now let us examine how each of these affects your ability to obtain the mortgage you want.

Down Payment

In spite of what you may have learned from books, newspapers and at real estate seminars, "nothing down" deals are extremely rare. Your chances of finding and putting together a deal that requires no down payment are slim. Virtually all home buyers put down anywhere from 10% to 25% of the purchase price while obtaining financing for the balance.

Here are the two basic variations in down payment you'll run into:

1. You make a down payment of 20 percent of the purchase price and borrow 80 percent from a bank or an S&L. If the purchase price of the house is $125,000, you'll come up with a down payment of $25,000 and your first mortgage will be in the amount of $100,000.

2. You may also put together a deal where the seller of the property provides a certain amount of financing. These are so-called "80-10-10" deals. In the example cited above, your down payment will be $12,500 and the seller will carry a note in the like amount, usually for a short duration of three to five years. The primary mortgage will be for 80% of the purchase price, generally for 30 years.

As a rule, your ability to qualify for a mortgage loan will be better with a higher down payment. The lender figures that with a greater down payment you'll have more at stake in making regular monthly mortgage payments.

Observation: Some lenders offer "no-qualifying" loans if you make a down payment of at least 25 percent. If you have the cash for such a deal, go for it. You'll save yourself a great deal of time and paperwork, not to mention the interest over the life of the loan.

Credit History

Next to the down payment you intend to make on the property, the lender would want to look at your track record of paying back past debts. A lender will order a credit report on you. Any delinquencies, late payments, defaults or judgments will be black mark against your credit worthiness and may be cause for credit denial.

A lender likes to see a borrower who has been paying back his debts on time. If you have been in the habit of paying for your purchases in cash, this may be a good time to quit that habit. Our credit conscious society almost requires you to incur some debts. A credit report that shows no history of borrowing may be just as bad as one that shows delinquencies. With no credit history, a lender cannot judge your past performance and predict how you'll fare in the future.

Ability to Repay

Finally, in determining how big a mortgage you can afford, a lender will look at your current income. Your monthly income has to be sufficiently high to service all your debts and still have money left over for the necessaries of life and other discretionary spending.

Different lenders use different formulas for arriving at the critical ratio. As a rule of thumb, your total monthly payment cannot exceed 36 percent of your total monthly income. In figuring your total monthly payment, the lender will look at:

● Mortgage principal and interest

● Property taxes

● Insurance

● Other long-term debts, such as car payment, other loans, credit card payments, etc.

In addition to this basic formula, the lender also makes allowance for the size of the down payment you're making. Here are two rules, and you may want to do some calculation on your part before settling down on the range of properties you should look at.

✓ **If your down payment is 10% of the purchase price, your monthly payment (PITI) cannot exceed 29 percent of** your monthly income.

✓ **If your down payment is 20% of the purchase price, your monthly payment (PITI) cannot exceed 33 percent of your monthly income.**

Illustration: Say your monthly income is $3,200. If you make a down payment of 10%, your mortgage payment for PITI will have to be limited to $928. By increasing your down payment to 20%, you can increase the mortgage payment for PITI to $1,056. This may make the difference in your being able to qualify for a certain property or not.

Recommendation: If you find that your monthly income falls shy of the mortgage you need to qualify for a particular home you have in mind, look for an adjustable rate mortgage. Lenders generally offer a lower introductory interest rate for an ARM and they base their qualifying on this lower rate. You may qualify with an ARM whereas you may not with a fixed rate loan. But also keep in mind that the introductory rate is just that; within six months to a year, you'll be paying the going rate and your mortgage payments will be adjusted to what they normally would have been.

Recommendation: If you still find that under your present financial circumstances your dream house is beyond your reach, look at a graduated payment mortgage (GPM). Under such a mortgage, your first year payments could be as much as 25% below the level payment required under a 30-year conventional mortgage. Every year, for the next five years, your payments will gradually rise at a rate ranging from 2% to 7.5%. After five years, for the remaining term of the loan, the payments will remain fixed at a level that would be higher than what would have been under a fixed-rate conventional loan.

In the first five years of the mortgage, your payments are not sufficient to fully amortize the loan; so for the remaining 25 years your payments have to be higher to make up for the unpaid interest. But without such a mortgage many home buyers would never be able to afford a home.

A GPM is ideal for individuals who expect to see their income rise substantially over the next few years as they reach the peak in their productive careers. GPM is also attractive to those who expect to move within a few years. Presumably the appreciation in the value of the house would take care of the negative amortization. For more complete discussion of this subject, see the chapter on **Graduated Payment Mortgages** in this book.

Lenders' Criteria in Evaluating a Loan Application

Although each lender has its own criteria on whether to approve or disapprove a particular loan application and this criteria may change from time to time, we have listed below a set of guidelines that most lenders use in evaluating your loan application. Under each category, the loan application may be graded with a plus or minus point. However, there are no hard and fast rules, and you must remember that there's room for negotiations in obtaining a mortgage from a lender.

Employment

Plus:

- Long-term steady employment
- Regular raises in income or salary
- Job changes or promotions which improve your salary or job status
- Possibility of future promotions
- Large, stable, well-known employer

Minus:

- Frequent job changes or job hopping
- High percentage of income from "other sources" such as commissions, bonuses, outside work, part-time work or consultations; unverifiable income
- Large fluctuations in income over the past several years
- Having just started a new business
- Excessive moonlighting

Financial

Plus:

- Large down payment; the larger the better
- A good credit history showing repayment of previous loans on schedule
- Substantial savings
- Substantial other assets (securities, stocks, car, other real estate, furniture, jewelry, collectibles, etc.)

Minus:
- Little cash savings, or cash reserve
- Bad debts history, such as late payments, delinquencies, or judgments
- Heavy, long-term debt load
- No previous borrowings

Property

Plus:
- Good location, in an up-scale neighborhood with potential appreciation in value
- A new well-kept home

Minus:
- Rundown neighborhood
- Non-conforming property
- Fixer-upper, requiring major repairs, especially with structural defects

Borrower

Plus:
- Young, married individual
- Well-educated professional
- Between the age of twenty-five to forty-five

Minus:
- Unskilled laborer
- Young people with no extensive job history
- Unmarried individuals

Appraisal of Home Values

Very often home owners wonder how their particular home is appraised by mortgage lenders or by FHA administration for purposes of lending money. The appraisals generally are conducted by certified appraisers in the area. If you are borrowing money from a bank or a savings and loan association, they would employ their own appraisers and the values established by these appraisers would be used in writing the mortgage.

Comparable Sales

Basically appraisers use two criteria. The most important one is the recent sale prices of comparable homes in the area. This takes into account the location of the house and compares it with other homes that have similar number of bedrooms and baths, and that were built about the same time, by the same developer. The style, the aging condition of the house, and other amenities, such as a swimming pool, central air conditioning, roof condition, size of the yards, etc. are also compared. These factors and the sale prices of comparable homes in the area form the benchmark used by the appraisers to arrive at a fair market value of your home. They may review the sale activity over several months to look at comparable sales that may have occurred in your area.

Most real estate brokers have a computer system that is designed to summarize all the sales in a particular area that fit the specific characteristics of your particular home. For example, the computer may be instructed to pull all the sale transactions that happened in a particular price range for a three bedroom, two bath home in a specific tract. Based on these comparable sales it would be easy to determine the sale value of your home.

Replacement Cost

The second criteria that often is used by appraisers is the replacement cost of a home. In this method, the appraiser calculates the square footage of the home and then multiplies it by the current construction cost per square foot in that area. This method may or may not produce reliable and acceptable price value. After all, a fair market value is the value agreed upon by a seller and buyer in any arms length negotiation. For all practical purposes, home sale prices are set by looking at the comparable sales in a particular area.

Amount of Deposit

A question that arises in most homebuyers' minds while buying a home is the amount of good-faith deposit that they should put down at the time of contracting to buy the home.

The brokers and seller would lead you to believe that 10% of the sale price is the normal and customary deposit, but when house prices range anywhere from $200,000 to $500,000 in many areas of the nation, putting down 10% of the sale price would require you to come up with $20,000 to $50,000. To tie up this sum of money for the duration of escrow, which may range from 30 days to 90 days or even longer, would cost you a tidy sum in lost interest.

In such cases, your negotiating posture while buying the home should be to limit the size of your deposit to as little as possible. It is not uncommon to put no more than a thousand dollars, or maybe two thousand dollars, at the time the contract to buy a home is signed. The remaining down payment would not be furnished till the escrow on the home is closed. Depending on the state you live in, you may also be entitled to interest earned on the deposit made on the house for the duration of the escrow.

There is one additional consideration on limiting the size of deposit you may want to put down while buying the home. The process of closing the escrow may take anywhere from 30 to 90 days, or even longer. During this period, things may go wrong in your personal life or with your finances, or you may have second thoughts. In the event you want to back out of a sale, if your deposit is small, it would be much easier for you to walk away from the deal. If you have put down ten to forty thousand dollars as a deposit, it would make it almost impossible for you to walk away from the sale without making sure that you would get a complete refund of your deposit.

Loan Discrimination: What Can You Do?

There are various state and federal laws that prohibit discrimination in extending credit to a home buyer. The foremost of these laws is the Federal Equal Credit Opportunity Act. The law makes it illegal to deny a mortgage loan because of the borrower's race, color, religion, national origin, sex, marital status, or income from public assistance. There are many state laws that also prohibit denial of a mortgage because of the location of the property, a practice commonly called "red lining."

If you think your mortgage loan has been denied unfairly, your first step would be to contact the lender, ask for a supervisor, or a person in charge of the mortgage loan department. Tell the person in charge that you would like him to review your application and tell you exactly why your application was denied. Under the federal laws, the lender is required to tell you and give you reasons in writing why your application was denied.

If you feel that you are not getting a satisfactory response from the lender, you have several options of being heard by various state and federal agencies. Below is a list of various federal agencies where you may wish to lodge your complaint.

When the lender is a federally insured savings and loan association, you should write to:

Federal Home Loan Bank Board
1700 G Street, N.W.
Washington, D.C. 20552

When the lender is a federally insured national or state bank, write to:

Federal Deposit Insurance Corporation
550 17th Street N.W.
Washington, D.C. 20551

When the lender is a national bank, write to:

Comptroller of the Currency
490 L'enfant Plaza
Washington, D.C. 20219

When the lender is a bank holding company or a state chartered commercial bank that is a member of the Federal Reserve System, write to:

Board of Governors
The Federal Reserve System
21st Street & Constitution Ave.
Washington, D.C. 20551

In most cases, a call or a personal visit to the lending institution will quickly right an obvious wrong. However, in some cases you may have to take your complaint to higher authorities.

Types of Mortgages at a Glance   3

Fixed Rate Mortgage

Until recently this was the workhorse of the mortgage industry. Most new mortgages without exception were fixed rate mortgages. As the name implies, the interest rate remains fixed throughout the life of the mortgage. It gives the borrower a sense of security that his mortgage payments will remain the same no matter what happens to the general economic conditions. As long as he is able to make his monthly mortgage payments, he will not lose his home.

With the advent of adjustable rate mortgages, fixed rate mortgages have fallen into a slight disfavor with the lenders. The rates on fixed rate mortgages are generally higher and mortgages are not assumable by the new owner.

Adjustable Rate Mortgage

The interest rate fluctuates every six months, and in some cases on an annual basis. The rate moves in tandem with some generally acceptable economic index, such as Federal Reserve Bank or Home Loan Bank rate measuring the cost of funds. To provide some degree of security to the borrower, there usually is a cap beyond which the interest rate would not rise. In addition, there may also be restrictions on the rate and payment increases from one period to the next. The flip side of this protection is that the loan may accrue negative amortization. In other words, you may actually owe the lender more down the road than you originally started out with.

Lenders have tried to make adjustable rate mortgages more attractive by offering lower than market interest rates at the beginning. This rate is then adjusted upwards after six months. Adjustable rate mortgages are generally easy to obtain and qualify for. They also are assumable by a qualified subsequent buyer of the property.

Balloon Mortgage

This generally is used only as a source of secondary financing. The mortgage is for a very short term, between three to five years. It may require only interest payment per month with the principal all due and payable at the end of the term of the loan. The balloon payment would actually be the amount borrowed.

The balloon mortgages were widely offered by anxious sellers during the days of astronomical interest rates when buyers found it hard to qualify for the entire purchase price with a traditional lender. The balloon loan was supposed to get the buyer in the house and tide him over till such time as he was able to procure more reasonable, long-term financing.

The biggest pitfall of balloon mortgages is that the borrower has to face the reality of having to come up with a very large sum of money within a few short years. Many homeowners have failed to come up with the balloon payment and had the house foreclosed upon them. You must approach a balloon mortgage only with a great deal of caution. If you do obtain a balloon mortgage, be sure to line up alternate financing sufficiently ahead of time.

Rollover Mortgage

This is similar to a balloon mortgage. The mortgage is written for a short term, usually five years, after which the borrower is required to roll over to another mortgage. The lender may sometimes guarantee to provide another mortgage at the then-prevailing interest rate, but otherwise the borrower is left with a possibility of costly, even unavailable financing at that time. Avoid such mortgages at all costs.

Graduated Payment Mortgage

This mortgage was created to make it easier for a first-time buyer to qualify for a home loan during relatively high interest rate periods. Under such a program, the first-year mortgage payments may be as much as 25% below those required under a conventional loan. For the next few years (3, 5 or 10) the payments gradually rise to the normal level so that for the remaining term of the loan they will remain level at a fixed sum.

Such a mortgage works best for those individuals who expect to see their earning capacity rise in the future years to keep pace with the higher mortgage payments. The biggest drawback of graduated payment mortgage is that it invariably produces negative amortization during the early years of the loan. If you plan to sell your house in a short time, you may have to pay off a loan that is in fact larger than when taken out.

Assumable Mortgage

This is an attractive feature in any mortgage and you should do everything possible to make sure that your mortgage is assumable by a new buyer of your home. Assumability of a mortgage will make it easier to market your home when the time comes. Normally, adjustable rate mortgages are assumable to qualified buyers, but fixed rate mortgages have a "due on sale" clause.

Seller Financed Mortgage

This is a creature of creative financing and is used widely during times when money is tight and interest rates too high. Seller, anxious to sell his home, would agree to provide part or whole of financing in the form of a first or second trust deed, often at less than market rates. The loan may require only interest payments and would be due and payable within three to five years.

For new homeowners, and also for real estate investors, seller-backed financing is the cheapest and most desirable source of money. You must use it at every opportunity even when traditional sources of money are available.

Portable Mortgage

A new kind of mortgage may be on the horizon, called portable mortgage. It is presently being marketed by Chase Home Mortgage Corporation. It allows home owners to take their mortgages with them when they move. You can lock in a fixed rate for fifteen or thirty years, with no limit on the number of moves. When you make a move to a home of comparable value, you will be able to take your current mortgage with you to the new home. The transfer fee charged by the bank is only five hundred dollars which is considerably less than typical points charged by a lender while obtaining a new mortgage.

If you move to a more expensive home and you need to borrow a larger sum of money, you would pay the prevailing rate on the additional sum and carry the previous portable mortgage with you. Your closing costs would be based only on the additional sum borrowed. This would still be cheaper than obtaining a new loan on the entire price of the house.

The portable mortgage rate is 1/4 of a percent higher than on Chase's conventional mortgage rate. The portable mortgage is presently available in about 38 states, including New York, New Jersey, California, and Florida. You would need to inquire and ask around to find if the banks in your area offer portable mortgages. If this instrument catches popularity it may be marketed more aggressively by other lenders.

Mortgage Checklist

4

1. Type of mortgage:

   _____   Conventional, 30-year, fixed rate

   _____   Adjustable rate mortgage (ARM)

   _____   FHA, VA mortgage

   _____   Biweekly mortgage

   _____   15-year mortgage

   _____   Graduated payment mortgage

2. Is there a loan application fee? If so, how much?

   $_____

3. Is there a property appraisal fee? How much?

   $_____

4. Is there a credit report fee? How much?

   $_____

5. What is the minimum down payment required by the
    lender?

    _____ percent of the purchase price

    $_____

6. How many points would the lender require to make the
    loan?
    _____, or $_____

7. Is there a prepayment penalty clause in the contract? How
    much of a principal can be repaid without incurring
    prepayment penalty? Is the penalty waived after a certain
    period?

    _____

8. Is there a "due-on-sale" clause?

    _____

9. Is the loan assumable by the new buyer of the property?
    On what terms?

    _____

10. Is there any seller-provided financing? Describe the terms.

    _____

11. If this is an adjustable rate mortgage:

(a) What is the introductory interest rate?

_____

(b) How long will this interest rate be in effect?

_____

(c) If interest rate is related to an index, which index will it be?

_____

(d) What is the margin on the ARM loan?

_____

(e) What is the interest rate cap?

_____

(f) Does the interest rate cap apply to the introductory (and lower) rate or to the rate in effect after the introductory period is over?

(g) What is the monthly payment cap?

_____

(h) How often can the adjustment be made in interest or payments? Every six months? Once a year?

_____

(i) What is the maximum adjustment that can be made in interest or payments each adjustment period?

_____

(j) Is there any negative amortization?

_____

(k) In the event of negative amortization, would the loan be "re-cast" after, say, five years to allow full amortization?

_____

(l) Is the loan assumable by a new qualified buyer? On what terms?

_____

12. What is the monthly payment including principal and interest?

$_____

13. What is the estimated taxes and insurance per month?

$_____

14. Does the lender require an impound account for payment of taxes and insurance?

_____

15. Would the lender require private mortgage insurance (PMI) coverage? What would be the cost of PMI?

_____

16. Could the PMI requirement be removed once the principal has been sufficiently paid down?

_____

17. How long will the mortgage loan commitment be effective?

_____

18. Will the interest rate remain fixed upon loan commitment?

_____

Prepayment of Principal

5

How do you cut the cost of your mortgage? How do you own your home in fifteen or twenty years instead of the usual thirty years? Before you get into the actual mechanics of reducing your interest costs on a loan, you need to understand the principle behind compound interest.

Principle Behind Principal Prepayment

Most individuals simply find it incomprehensible how the principal prepayment works and the dramatic effect it has on the total interest cost of borrowing. Let me assure you that it's not as confusing as you might think. In fact, once you understand the concept of compound interest you'll realize that this entire area of financing upon which the bankers and mortgage lenders have built their empires is fairly easy to master and penetrate.

Compound Interest

Compound interest is nothing more than interest earned on interest. When you leave your money in a savings account, the principal earns interest at the rate stated by the bank. If you do not withdraw the interest earned, in the next period it too will earn interest and will continue do so in each successive period. In other words, interest is now computed not just on the principal amount, but on the principal and interest amounts combined. When you repeat this process for each of the successive periods, you have the effect of compound interest.

Illustration: Say you've deposited $20 in your savings account at 11% a year. By letting the interest to accumulate in the account, you are in effect getting the compound interest. At the end of the first year, your $20 principal has earned $2.20 in interest. Therefore, in the second year you'll earn interest not on $20 but on the combined sum of $22.20. Each year thereafter interest is earned on the ever-increasing principal so that at the end of five years your $20 has grown to $33.70. After 20 years, you'll have $161.20 in your account and at the end of 30 years, you'll have $457.85.

How Principal Prepayment Works

We saw above the concept of compounded interest in relation to your savings account. When you borrow money from a bank, the same principle works in reverse. Each month the bank computes the interest due on the outstanding balance of your loan. By prepaying all or part of the balance of the loan, you're avoiding interest charges on that sum.

For example, taking one extreme, by paying off the entire mortgage amount in the first month you'll incur no interest charge at all. By prepaying a partial balance due, you're eliminating interest cost on that amount month after month, throughout the duration of the loan. By prepaying a small amount of the principal balance each month, you're constantly reducing the amount upon which the bank could charge the interest.

In other words, by making a prepayment you're saving all the compound interest the bank was planning to charge on that amount for the duration of the loan. Remember, prepayments are not additional costs; they are simply small amounts paid before they were due.

In this book we're going to show you several methods for reducing your mortgage cost. They are:

1. **Variable Sum Prepayment Plan**

2. **Fixed Sum Prepayment Plan**

3. **Fixed Term Prepayment Plan**

These plans work in very similar fashion and they all deliver fantastic savings. You can choose one or more, or even a combination of several plans. Personally, I favor the Fixed Term Prepayment Plan; it's extremely simple, requires no bookkeeping and allows you to set your own goal. You choose the length of the mortgage you desire and your payments are set to that term. But read the discussion below and then choose the plan that will work the best for you.

Variable Sum Prepayment Plan

In this plan, the amount of principal you'll be paying each month varies according to the loan amortization schedule. The amount to be prepaid would be the amount of principal due on your next payment and this will gradually increase each month.

Mortgage Amortization Schedule

Before you start out on this particular prepayment program, you'll need the mortgage amortization schedule applicable to your loan. This is easy to obtain from your lender, either a bank or mortgage institution. Your loan officer, the individual who helped you fill out the loan application and processed the loan, may be of help if you run into some bureaucratic resistance. Most banks will provide you with the mortgage amortization schedule as a matter of courtesy.

In addition, many people own financial calculators and personal computers. If you have access to such a computer, there are several software programs on the market that spew out amortization schedules by punching in relevant data.

Remember, your amortization schedule will be unique to your loan. Based upon the amount borrowed, interest rate charged and the term of the loan, it calculates the monthly payment necessary to fully amortize (i.e., pay off) the loan over the term. The amortization schedule takes your monthly payment and breaks it into two components, one going toward the interest and the other toward the principal. The last column in the schedule shows the unpaid balance.

A mortgage amortization schedule is necessary so that you can determine each month the amount you need to prepay. Once you have started on this program and have made entries on the schedule that shows the amount of interest saved, it will give you a tremendous sense of satisfaction and achievement as you travel toward that goal of debt-free ownership of your home.

In the illustration below, we show you how the method works. The amount of the principal that you'll be prepaying each month will vary; in fact, it will be gradually increasing as you progress along the term of the loan. By looking at the amortization schedule you'll be able to tell how much each prepayment of principal is saving you in interest expense.

How a Variable Sum Prepayment Plan Works

Variable Sum Prepayment Plan

Loan amount:	$75,000
Interest rate:	10.00%
Term (no. of monthly payments):	30 years, 360 payments
Monthly payment:	$658.18
Total interest, if not pre-paid:	$161,941.57
Principal borrowed:	$75,000.00
Total cash outlay:	$236,941.57

Payment No.	Interest	Principal	Unpaid Balance
1	$625.00	$33.18	$74,966.82
2	624.72	33.46	74,933.36
3	624.44	33.74	74,899.62
4	624.16	34.02	74,865.60
5	623.88	34.30	74,831.30
..	....	....	....
..	....	....	....
356	26.73	631.45	2,575.65
357	21.46	636.72	1,938.93
358	16.16	642.02	1,296.91
359	10.81	647.37	649.54
360	5.41	649.54	0.00

Illustration: We've prepared a partial amortization schedule for a sample loan as shown here. The loan amount is $75,000 amortized over 30 years at 10% interest rate. Monthly payment for such a loan would be $658.18 per month. The schedule shows the first and last five payments breaking them down between principal and interest. If this loan was paid off as structured, i.e., without making any prepayments, the total interest paid over 30 years would be $161,941.57, bringing the total cash outlay to $236,941.57.

By looking at our sample mortgage amortization table, you quickly notice that during the initial period a very large portion of your monthly payment goes toward interest. The amount of principal reduced in the first month of the loan is only $33.18 and then rises ever so slightly over the life of the loan so that toward the last part of the term a very large portion of your monthly payment is applied to reduce the principal.

As per your mortgage obligation, you're required to pay each monthly payment of $658.18 on time till the entire loan balance is paid in full. You could not pay less or skip any payments, but you could pay more.

You could start your prepayment program at any time during the term of the loan, but since during the earlier stages of the loan most of your payments are applied toward the interest you would achieve maximum savings by starting the prepayment plan as soon as possible.

Let's say you are about to send in your first mortgage payment to the bank, in this case in the amount of $658.18. At this time you could add the principal payment of second month ($33.46) to your regular payment of $658.18, thereby sending a total of $691.64. You may send two separate checks, one in the amount of $658.18 and the other in the amount of $33.36 indicating how to apply each of these checks, or you could send one check in the total sum of $691.64 with a note that indicates how you wish to apply the total payment. I suggest you contact the loan service department of your bank and ask them how they would prefer to receive such a payment. In most cases, banks have no preference as long as your instructions are clear as to how you wish your money to be applied.

If you follow the practice of sending in one prepayment check with each regular mortgage payment, you'll cut the life of the mortgage in half. You'll own your home in 15 years instead of 30 years.

To continue with our example, by making that extra payment of $33.46 you've saved yourself $624.72 in interest cost associated with the second payment. You'll never have to pay that $624.72. Next month when you send in your regular monthly payment of $658.18 it will be credited to payment #3 since you already have paid off the principal due during the second month. If you're to continue your prepayment plan, you would also send in an extra payment of $34.02 which is the principal due in month #4 thereby saving another $624.16. By making two extra payments of $67.48, you've saved yourself $1,248.88 in interest charges.

But this is not all. By making those two extra payments of principal, you also have loped two months off the life of your loan. You'll own your home debt-free so much sooner.

There is one thing to remember. Under the terms of your loan, you are obliged to make at least one payment of $658.18 each month. You have to do this till the entire loan is paid off. You are not obliged to send in the extra payments we have talked about here. If, for some reason, you are not in a position to prepay any month, that's fine. If, however, you have some extra cash any month, you could send that in to prepay the principal and save several times in interest cost.

By paying off the mortgage several years sooner than its original term of 30 years, you'll then have extra cash left over to use in any manner you wish. That's the pay-off. And it's a big pay-off. Your prepayment of $33.46 in the first month alone has brought you savings of $624.72, a return of 1,867%. I know of no other investment that will even remotely produce such a return.

Tracking Your Prepayments

This is where the fun begins. We've now seen how small prepayments mushroom into large savings. Keeping track of these savings is the exciting part of this program. You are charting your progress toward that debt-free ownership of your home and soon you'll discover that your 30-year term has been cut into only 15 years and there are no more mortgage payments to make. It is an exhilarating thought.

What's is more important, you're still in the prime of your life. Most people own their home free and clear when they are nearing retirement. They have practically worked all their life to own that home. In your case, you may be able to enjoy your home and the tremendous savings long before you retire.

How do you keep track of the progress you're making in paying off the mortgage? Using the same example illustrated above, we've prepared an amortization table with columns to enter the prepayments and interest saved. After you have obtained your mortgage amortization table from your lender, you may want to prepare a similar table on any columnar worksheet. Each month you'll enter your payments here.

The amortization table will provide you with the payment no., interest, principal and unpaid balance amounts. Enter these amounts on your worksheet. If it is a 30-year loan, you'll have payments starting from 1 to 360. If you're starting this prepayment program sometime after the inception of the loan, you'll have fewer remaining payments. In any case, your worksheet should show the remaining payments broken down between interest and principal.

Say your first payment is due on January 1. You have decided to make one prepayment of principal attributed to the month of February. You would enter Jan. 1 in the Date Paid column for Payment #1 and #2; in the Amount Paid column for January, you'll enter $658.18 and for February you'll enter $33.46. You'll also enter $624.72 in the Interest Saved column for February; this is the amount you've saved by making the prepayment. The column entitled Total Interest Saved is merely a sum of interest saved in all the previous months as a result of your prepayments. This column shows you your total savings at a glance.

You would repeat the same process in February. Say you are in a position to make two extra prepayments. You are going to prepay the principal amounts attributed to the month of April and May, $34.02 and $34.30 respectively. These entries are shown in our sample worksheet. This is all there is to it. Each month as you get ready to pay your mortgage, bring out your mortgage amortization schedule, decide how much you are going to prepay, make appropriate entries, and watch your savings multiply. Nothing could be simpler.

Variable Sum Prepayment Plan Worksheet

Payment No.	Date Paid	Interest	Interest Saved	Total Interest Saved	Principal	Amount Paid	Unpaid Balance

When Do You Stop Making the Prepayments?

Here is something to keep in mind. As you pass the mid-term point of your loan, you realize that your prepayments are getting larger and they are not saving you quite as much in interest as the earlier payments did. This is so because now a greater portion of your payment goes toward satisfying principal and proportionately smaller portion toward interest. Also, your prepayments are no longer small amounts; they have far outgrown the "spare change" status. You may want to cut back on your prepayments at this stage. The choice is yours. We'll talk more about this consideration later in the book.

Fixed Sum Prepayment Plan

Our previous discussion on prepayment strategy centered on prepaying a variable sum each month. This sum was determined from the mortgage amortization table and represented the principal due on the next payment. This amount varied each month. In fact, it grew gradually each month as more and more of your monthly payment was applied to the principal.

The major drawback with this plan is that after a few years the principal amount no longer remains a small sum. It becomes gradually larger with each payment, and some point along the way you may find that coming up with the monthly mortgage and the prepayment sum is not an easy job. Prepaying is no longer fun; it has turned into a daunting task.

If you prefer, there is another prepayment method available to you. Under this plan, your prepayments are fixed in sum each month. Let us say you are able to save and send in $25 each month as prepayment of principal of your loan. This is a fairly small amount and would pose no hardship on anyone. In fact, it is less than the cost of a dinner out for two. If you can add this paltry sum to your regular monthly mortgage payment, you'll be able to stockpile savings in interest that will astound you.

Some people may prefer to use this Fixed Sum Prepayment Plan to the Variable Sum Plan simply because they know exactly how much more they are going to pay in advance each month. There are no decisions to make. This plan may also have a psychological advantage in that since you are not making that monthly decision of making the extra prepayment you may not feel the burden of parting with the cash. Fixed Sum Prepayment Plan has the inertial force built into it; it simply propels you toward

your goal of debt-free ownership of home. Put it another way, it
is as if your mortgage payments were fixed arbitrarily at a slightly
higher level, and you were not told about it. It is a pleasant and
profitable way of deceiving yourself.

Keeping Track of Fixed Sum Prepayments

Bookkeeping under the Fixed Sum Prepayment Plan is
also relatively easy. First, you determine exactly how much more
you would like to prepay each month. This may be $25, $35, $50
or $100. It could be any amount you feel you could prepay without
stretching your finances and budget unduly. Once you have
determined this amount, simply ask your bank or lender to supply
you with a mortgage amortization table based on the new monthly
payment figure. When you receive this amortization table, you'll
be pleasantly surprised that several years have been loped off your
original term of the loan of 30 years. Depending upon the amount
you have chosen to prepay, your mortgage will be paid off five, ten
or even more years sooner than planned.

To illustrate the Fixed Sum Prepayment Plan, we have
recalculated the amortization schedule of the loan in our earlier
example. It includes a prepayment of $25 per month raising the
monthly payment to $683.18. This in turn reduces the term of the
loan by 63 months saving $34,162.09 in interest cost.

Fixed Sum Prepayment Plan

Loan Amount:	75,000.00
Interest Rate:	10.00%
Term (Monthly Payments):	297
Months Saved by Prepayment:	63
Base Monthly Payment:	658.18
Regular Prepayment:	25.00
Total Monthly Payment:	683.18
Total Interest, If Not Prepaid:	161,941.57
Total Interest, if Prepaid:	127,779.48
Interest Saved by Regular Prepayment:	34,162.09
Total Outlay Without Prepayment:	236,941.57
Total Outlay With Prepayment:	202,779.48

Payment	Interest	Principal	Balance
1	625.00	58.18	74,941.82
2	624.52	58.66	74,883.16
3	624.03	59.15	74,824.01
4	623.53	59.65	74,764.36
5	623.04	60.14	74,704.22
6	622.54	60.64	74,643.58

Fixed Term Prepayment Plan

We've discussed two kinds of prepayment plans so far. There is yet another way to devise your prepayment plan which you might find more attractive. Here's how it works.

Let's say you have a $100,000 conventional 30-year mortgage at 9.25%. Your monthly payments are $822.68 and, by looking up in the mortgage tables, you can determine that you'll be paying $196,165 in total interest over the life of the loan. Your goal is to cut down the life of the mortgage from 30 years to, say, 25 years, or 20 years, or 15 years. How much prepayment of principal would be required under each of these scenarios? There are financial tables readily available in many stationery stores which will provide you with answers.

Fixed Term Prepayment Plan

| Amount of Loan: | $100,000 |
| Interest rate: | 9.25% |

Term of Loan	Monthly Payment	Total Interest	Interest Saved
30 years	$ 822.68	$196,165	-
25 years	856.39	156,917	$ 39,248
20 years	915.87	119,809	76,356
15 years	1,029.20	85,256	110,909

Now you can choose the amount of monthly payment you feel comfortable with and that will determine the speed with which you'll be able to own your home debt-free. If you can spare about $35 a month, you would be able to take five years off the life of the mortgage. Prepaying an extra $206.52 per month will allow you to cut the life of the mortgage in half.

This approach to prepaying has the advantage of simplicity to it. You do not need to obtain amortization schedules nor do you have to determine the amount to be prepaid each month. Once you have determined the length of the mortgage, your monthly payments are fixed. This, of course, is true only with the conventional fixed-rate mortgages. With adjustable rate mortgages, you'll have to change your payments every time there is an adjustment in the interest rate.

Where do you find the financial tables you need for this method? We've a couple of sources for you:

Consumer Guide to Mortgage Payments
Financial Publishing Company
82 Brookline Avenue
Boston. Mass 02215
(617) 262-4040

How to Save Thousands of Dollars on Your Mortgage
Michael Sherman, Ph.D.
Contemporary Books, Inc.
180 North Michigan Avenue
Chicago, IL 60601

Your Questions Answered About Prepayment

6

The Myth of Prepayment Penalty

Here's is one of the most common objections you'll hear to our program of prepaying the principal to save hundreds of thousands of dollars in interest:

"Yes, but my lender will impose a prepayment penalty."

This is nothing more than a myth. People who raise the specter of prepayment penalty obviously have not thought through the situation. They have heard of prepayment penalty and they assume that it's going to stop them from reaping the benefits of prepayments. Nothing could be farther from truth.

Let's put the problem into proper perspective.

1. A great number of loans simply do not have any prepayment penalty. This is all the more true with a majority of loans written in recent years. If your loan happens to be an adjustable rate loan, it almost certainly will not have any prepayment penalty. Therefore, check your loan contract carefully to see if there is any prepayment penalty.

2. If you have an FHA or VA mortgage, it generally cannot have a prepayment penalty. So if you've one of these kinds of mortgages, you're free to prepay the mortgage with few restrictions. Again, read your mortgage contract.

3. An increasing number of states have adopted legislation that does away with any restrictions on a mortgagor's option to prepay his loan. Even if your loan calls for prepayment penalties, it's possible that the law will prevent the lender from collecting any penalties. (Courts are finding that mortgages that contain "due on sale" clauses and prepayment penalties are simply inconsistent and is an example of overreaching by the mortgagees. A lender has to choose between one or the other. It cannot have its cake and eat it too.)

4. Now let's take the case where the mortgage contract does call for a prepayment penalty. Again, read the clause carefully. In most cases this penalty applies only if you prepay more than 20% of the original loan amount in any twelve month period. Now follow this: The 20% is in addition to the regular monthly payments you're obligated to make. For prepayments exceeding the 20% limit, the penalty is in the form of 120- to 180-day interest on that excess amount.

As you'll see in just a minute, this is nothing to worry about. Let's take, for example, a $120,000 conventional loan at 11% interest for 30 years. Your monthly loan payments would amount to $1,142.79. In order to incur a prepayment penalty, you would have to prepay $24,000 in principal. This is in addition to $13,713.48 of your regular payments during the 12-month period.

For all practical purposes, few homeowners would be in a position to come up with $37,713.48 in one year. The prepayment of principal program that we have described in this book calls for only small amounts of prepayments with money that you can afford to spare without straining your finances. It is highly unlikely that an average homeowner is going to run afoul of the prepayment penalty clause under these circumstances.

There is one more consideration. Many mortgages that impose prepayment penalty also provide for elimination of such a penalty after the first three or five years. Again, read your mortgage instrument and loan conditions carefully. Much to your surprise, you may find that, at this stage of your mortgage, the prepayment penalty does not apply to you.

Prepayment penalty is seldom the deterrent it is often made out to be. Do not let some preconceived notions stand between you and the tremendous savings awaiting you.

Would Prepayments Make It Harder For You to Sell the House?

This is another fallacy entertained by many homeowners. They are under the impression that by making the prepayments and reducing the outstanding principal they would make the sale of the house so much more difficult. This simply isn't so. In fact, the new buyer as well as you stand to profit from a lower loan balance. Here's how.

Let's assume that you've owned the house for about five years, and you've been making regular monthly prepayments of $50 on your loan of $125,000 at 11% interest. Your prepayments during these five years have reduced the principal by $3,000, saved a whopping amount in interest costs and knocked several months off the term of your loan.

Now when you go to sell your house, your equity is higher by $3,000 than it would have been if you had not made any prepayments. If a prospective buyer decides to obtain a new loan, you'll be fully compensated for your prepayments. The buyer's new loan proceeds will pay off the balance remaining on the current loan and you'll receive the difference between that and the sale price.

If you've been making prepayments for only a few years, the reduction in principal isn't going to be significant. If your prepayments were made for a longer period of time, your equity has increased considerably. In either case, the buyer's new loan will compensate you for your prepayments.

Now let's assume that your present mortgage is assumable by a buyer. Your prepayments will actually provide you with additional firepower in your sales effort. The buyer of your property is going to benefit from your prepayments. He'll save thousands of dollars in interest costs and he will own his house several years sooner as a direct result of your prepayments. Instead of a 30-year mortgage, he may be looking at a 20- or 25-year mortgage. This makes your house so much more attractive for him to buy. In fact, with the help of a competent and knowledgeable broker, you may be able to command a higher price than a comparable house without such a benefit. Interest saved through prepayments on an assumable loan is an extremely powerful selling tool.

Will the Prepayments Affect My Taxes?

Mortgage interest deduction holds a special lure for many homeowners. In essence, Uncle Sam is subsidizing your home purchase by allowing you to deduct the interest paid on your income tax return. If you're in the 28% income tax bracket, every dollar of interest paid actually costs you only 72 cents. Even under the new tax reform law the mortgage interest deductibility has been left untouched.

Now the question is: Will the prepayments of principal affect the amount of taxes you pay? The answer is, your prepayments of principal will have only a negligible effect on your interest deduction and the taxes paid. Remember, you are still required to make regular monthly payments whether you prepay or not. The interest charge on these twelve monthly mortgage payments will total almost the same with or without prepayments. Although you are piling up huge savings in total interest costs over the term of the loan, your monthly interest cost is decreasing only very slowly.

Illustration: Take for instance a $75,000 30-year loan at 10%. If you do not prepay, your mortgage interest deduction during the first year of the loan would be $7,481.24. If you prepay $25 per month, your tax deductible interest amount would be reduced by $14.12 to $7,467.12. In your 28% tax bracket, you may end up paying $3.95 more in taxes in that year. But your savings in interest costs would amount to more than $5,000. As you see, the question of losing mortgage interest deduction on your income tax return is patently absurd.

Should I Prepay Even Though I Plan to Sell My House?

The prepayment program is most beneficial to those who plan to hold on to their home for a long time. If you intend to fully pay off the mortgage and plan to spend your retirement years in your home, your prepayments would make that dream a reality much sooner. Your interest savings would multiply and your mortgage could be cut in half as a result of your prepayments.

But what if you plan to sell your home in five years or less and move to another home? Obviously, your small prepayments aren't going to make a significant difference. You would, of course, save thousands of dollars in interest, but your principal balance would not go down significantly. As we said earlier, you are still going to get back the prepayments you've made from the buyer in the form of increased equity in the house when you sell it. If you reinvest the proceeds from the sale of this house to another, your new loan would be so much smaller, and mortgage payments correspondingly smaller.

Therefore, keep this in mind. If you intend to hold on to the house for a long time, and possibly even pay off the mortgage in full, you'll have saved a tremendous amount with your prepayments. If you plan to sell your house after a short time, your benefit may not be as great, but you'll save nonetheless.

When Should I Start on the Prepayment Plan?

You can start prepaying your principal any time you wish. However, from our previous discussion, you must now have realized that the greatest savings in interest occur at the beginning of the term of loan. At this stage, a very small percent of your monthly payment goes toward reducing the principal, rest going toward interest. For each successive month the interest paid decreases and the principal retired increases by the like sum. This process continues throughout the life of the loan until toward the end of the loan the situation just reverses. Last few payments on your loan would go mostly toward the principal.

If you look at the amortization schedule of your mortgage, you'll be struck by the fact that monthly interest payments remain large for many years. In our example, after making monthly mortgage payments of $658.18 for ten years, your 121st payment still contains $568.36 in interest and only $89.82 in principal. By this time you already have paid back $78,981.60 (120 times $658.18) - a sum that is larger than that borrowed. If this is not enough to floor you, consider this: you still have twenty more years of payments to make.

The purpose of this discussion is to bring home the point that even if you have owned your home for several years and been making regular monthly payments (partly because no one ever told you about the magical savings achieved from principal prepayments,) it's not too late. You can still start on the prepayment program and start accruing significant savings.

Things may, however, change toward the end of the loan. At this stage it may not make much sense to prepay a large principal in order to save a small amount of interest. You might just want to stay with your regular monthly mortgage payments till the loan is paid off. In fact, by making these large principal prepayments you may only be helping your lender or bank. They'll be anxious to close your loan which is earning hardly any interest and lend the money to a new borrower from whom they can start collecting the high interest all over.

What Kind of Loans Can Be Prepaid?

Our discussion in this book has concentrated on home mortgage loans. For virtually all individuals, this represents the biggest investment they are ever going to make. Due to the large amount borrowed and length of the loan, prepayment program yields the greatest savings when applied to home mortgages. But this by no means restricts the use of prepayment options to home mortgages alone.

You can use prepayment plans in any type of loan whether it is an auto or boat loan, home improvement loan, student loan, bill consolidation loan or even a signature loan where you are borrowing without collateral. Here's the rule of thumb: The larger the amount borrowed, the greater the interest and longer the term of the loan, the more you'll save with each prepayment of principal.

There's one kind of loan that cannot be repaid. These loans are so-called "Rule of 78" loans. The interest is computed on the sum of digits method with the front-loading of interest. In most states such loans have been outlawed. If you have any questions, you should check with your banker or lender. In fact, make it a rule to inquire about your right to prepay a loan before signing up for it.

What About Adjustable Rate Mortgages?

During the past few years banks and other mortgage institutions have responded to the high and unpredictable cost of money by offering adjustable rate mortgages. In an adjustable rate mortgage loan, a borrower is typically offered a very low initial rate (often called "teaser" rate) which is then adjusted upwards six or twelve months later. This rate fluctuates in tandem with one of the established cost of money indices. Often the lender will place a cap on the extent of fluctuation allowed from one period of adjustment to the next. This cap may be in the form of interest rate or the amount of mortgage payment, or a combination of both.

Your principal prepayment plan would work just as well with an adjustable rate mortgage as with any other conventional mortgage. You can prepay the principal either in a fixed amount or a variable amount each month and reap the tremendous savings in interest.

Your bookkeeping may be a little more complicated in an adjustable rate mortgage. Every time the interest rate or your mortgage payment changes, the mortgage amortization schedule will change too. In order to send in the exact amount of principal due on the next payment and to keep track of your savings to the penny, you'll need to obtain a new mortgage amortization schedule every time there's an adjustment in your mortgage. This would be inconvenient in most cases unless you have access to a personal computer with appropriate software to produce your amortization schedule.

If your prepayment plan calls for a fixed sum to be prepaid each month (say $25, $50 or $100) and you are not overly concerned about keeping track of your savings down to the last penny, you'll have no trouble with your adjustable rate mortgage.

Tip: During the life of your adjustable rate mortgage there will be some pleasant surprises sprung on you by your lender. The interest rates may actually have declined in the previous period and now your monthly payments for the next six or twelve months will be lower than current payments. What are you going to do? Are you going to treat this lower mortgage payment as a much-deserved raise and spend it? Or, would you rather continue to make the same payments that you have gotten used to making and apply the excess to the principal? The choice is, of course, yours.

15-Year vs. 30-Year Mortgage

7

For a long time almost all home mortgages were written for a 30-year term. Just as the 3-year auto loans were the norm until cars became so expensive that people began to amortize them over four years, 30-year home mortgages have been the accepted convention in this country since the World War II. That is, until recently. Many homeowners have discovered that they can save thousands of dollars in interest by cutting down on the length of the mortgage. In the last few years, many innovative banks and mortgage institutions have introduced a dizzying array of mortgages to fit the demands of the marketplace.

In some cases, this has been nothing more than a marketing ploy to capture the imagination of the public with a new, exciting product. But what about a 15-year mortgage? Does it offer some real benefits to the homeowner? Are there any pitfalls to this shorter term mortgage? Is it for everyone? We'll examine all these questions in this chapter.

How the Term Affects the Monthly Payment

It is apparent to even the most uninitiated borrower that the same amount borrowed over a longer term would entail smaller monthly payments. The critical question is, how much smaller, at what cost and, is there an optimum term for a mortgage loan?

Let's take the example of a $120,000 loan at 11% interest rate and examine the impact of the duration of the loan upon the monthly payments.

15-Year Mortgage vs. 30-Year Mortgage

$120,000 Mortgage at 11%

Term in years	Monthly Payment
5	$2,609.10
10	1,653.01
15	1,363.92
20	1,238.63
25	1,176.14
30	1,142.79
35	1,124.35
40	1,113.96

Needless to say, the longer the term, the smaller the payment. And since most home buyers look for the smallest monthly payment possible, they would generally opt for a more readily available conventional 30-year mortgage.

But why a 30-year mortgage? Why not 40-year or even 50-year mortgage?

The reason is obvious if you look at the chart that plots monthly mortgage payments on one axis and the term of the loan on another. As we go from 5 to 10 to 15 to 20 year mortgage, the reduction in monthly payment is very significant. In our example, the monthly payment on the $120,000 loan reduces from $2,609.10 for a 5-year mortgage to $1,653.01 for a 10-year term to $1,238.63 for a 20-year and approaches $1,142.79 at 30-year mark. Without a doubt, for a prospective homebuyer this is a critical consideration. He may not qualify for a 10-year loan at $1,653.01 monthly payment whereas he would easily qualify for a 30-year loan.

However, as we approach the 30-year term, we're reaching a plateau, an optimum point. As each year is added to the term of the loan, the reduction in monthly mortgage payment becomes increasingly smaller. To go from 30 years to 35 years, the monthly payments will go down only $18.44. But you have added five years to the life of the mortgage and increased the total cost of paying off the mortgage by $60,822.60. By going to a 40-year mortgage, you'll remain indebted for ten more years and pay $123,296.40 in additional money. This is why the curve gradually becomes flatter and we reach the point of diminishing returns.

Now you can appreciate why a 30-year mortgage has become the standard in the industry.

Why a 30-year Mortgage?

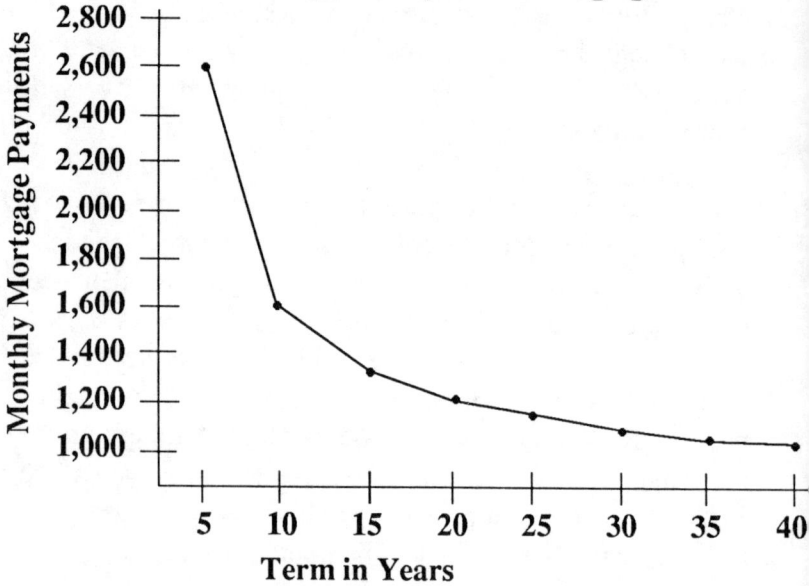

Monthly mortgage payments versus term of mortgage

Monthly payments decline dramatically as the term of the loan increases from 5 years to 30. After that, increasing the life of the loan brings only diminishing returns.

Savings With a 15-Year Mortgage

Now let us compare a 30-year mortgage with a 15-year mortgage.

Amount borrowed: $120,000
Interest rate: 10%

Term of Loan	Monthly Payment	Total Interest Cost	Interest Saved
30-year	$1,053.09	$259,112	—
15-year	$1,289.53	$112,115	$146,997

As we see from the above table, by going from a 30-year to 15-year mortgage you have increased your monthly payment by $236.44, but have reduced the total interest paid by $146,997. Your total interest cost over the life of the mortgage has gone down by more than 50%. These dramatic savings in interest are achieved because you're borrowing money over a shorter period of time. In fact, under a 15-year mortgage, the portion of your monthly payment that is applied toward principal is several times the amount under a 30-year mortgage.

Traps of a 15-year Mortgage

If a 15-year mortgage saves so much money, shouldn't everyone go for it?

But before you rush out and sign up for a 15-year mortgage on your home, you should be aware of certain traps. The biggest trap is, of course, the higher monthly payment. Generally speaking, you would need higher income to qualify for a 15-year mortgage as opposed to a 30-year mortgage. Your payments would be approximately 22% higher with the shorter mortgage. The lender would like to see that your salary and other income are sufficient to justify this increased burden. In some cases, a home buyer would simply not be able to qualify for a 15-year mortgage whereas he would for a 30-year mortgage.

A 15-year mortgage carries with it a potential future problem. It is possible that you are currently able to afford this higher mortgage, but there is no guarantee that you'll continue to have the same earnings at all times in the future. In fact, over the life of that mortgage there may come a time when those higher payments will become a real burden. Maybe there is an illness in the family, maybe you've lost a high-paying job, or you're facing some unexpected expenses. Your inability to make timely mortgage payments may cause you to default on your loan and force the lender to foreclose on the loan. At times like these you would wish that you had never heard of a 15-year mortgage.

But there's no need to despair. You can get all the benefits of a 15-year mortgage and still avoid potential traps associated with it. You can have your cake and eat it too. Here's how.

15-Year Mortgage With None of Its Traps

The solution to the above-described dilemma lies in your ability to prepay the principal on your mortgage. These days most loans permit prepayment of principal without penalty. Check your loan documents and verify that there's no prepayment penalty. Also, read the section on prepayment penalty in this book. Now follow the example below.

Illustration: Say you have a 30-year $120,000 mortgage at 10% interest rate. Your monthly payment is $1,053.09. You would like to have the option of paying off this mortgage in 15 years without locking yourself in higher payments for the entire term of the loan. What's the solution?

Each month you include with your regular payment an extra sum of $236.44 and instruct your lender to apply that sum to the principal of the loan. (You arrive at this figure by looking up in your mortgage tables the payment necessary to fully amortize the $120,000 loan at 10% over 15 years which happens to be $1,289.53, and subtracting from it the payment required on the 30-year mortgage.) If you are able to do this each month for the next fifteen years, you'll have a debt-free home at the end of fifteen years. In essence, you've cut your mortgage in half.

What if you run into some financial hot water at some time in the future and are unable to make that extra payment?

No problem. You are under no obligation to continue with the prepayment plan. You can stop your prepayment plan at any time you wish. If things improve and you're able to resume your prepayments, you'll start to reduce your mortgage again. In any case, your mortgage will be of less than 30-year duration. You have achieved the dual goal of cutting down on your mortgage without burdening yourself with the dangerously high monthly payments for the entire life of the mortgage.

The 40-Year Mortgage: Avoid It

We've just seen that 30 years is probably the optimum life term of a mortgage. What if the money becomes very scarce and you find it hard to qualify for a conventional 30-year mortgage? Should you accept a 40-year mortgage if it's offered to you? Your answer in unequivocal terms should be, no. Here's why.

Illustration: Take for instance an $85,000 mortgage loan at 10%. Let us compare this loan at three different terms: 15 years, 30 years and 40 years.

The table below shows you that at 15-year term, you'll be paying $167.47 more per month over the 30-year mortgage, but you'll pay off the mortgage in half the time and save $104,123.10 in interest costs over the life of the mortgage. On the other hand, a 40-year mortgage, as compared to a 30-year mortgage, will reduce your monthly payments by $24.17, but bind you to your mortgage for ten more years at an additional interest cost of $77,912.70.

Is this worth it? My advice is to forget about it. Wait till you can afford a few more dollars a month in mortgage payments, or find a house you can realistically afford at this time.

Loan Comparison by Term

Loan term	15 years	30 years	40 years
Loan size	$85,000	$85,000	$85,000
Interest rate	10 percent	10 percent	10 percent
Number of payments	180	360	480
Monthly payment	$913.41	$745.94	$721.77
Monthly cost differential	+$167.47	-	−$24.17
Balloon payment	-	-	-
Total potential interest	$79,413.80	$183,536.90	$261,449.60
Interest differential	- $104,123.10	-	+$77,912.70

Biweekly Mortgage 8

Until recently few lenders offered biweekly mortgages. They were just a lot of nuisance, costly to service and full of bookkeeping headaches. However, several recent developments may hasten their acceptance around the country. First, let's see how a typical biweekly mortgage works.

How a Biweekly Mortgage Works

In a biweekly mortgage, a borrower makes 26 payments in a year to the lender as opposed to 12 monthly payments in a conventional loan. Each payment is, however, only half the size of the regular monthly payment. In other words, the borrower is making one extra monthly payment each year. As a result, the interest costs are reduced, the loan term is shortened and the borrower owns the home so much sooner.

Biweekly mortgages are especially popular with some individuals who get paid every other week; it allows them to coincide their mortgage payments with their paydays.

Each lender uses its own particular "daily basis" method of computing accrued interest on the biweekly mortgages. Typically the lender takes the annual simple interest rate and divides it by the daily basis of either 360, 364 or 365 to come up with the daily interest factor. Lenders who use 365 day basis earn slightly less interest than lenders who earn 360 day basis, and thus their mortgage terms are shorter. We'll use only 365 day basis in our discussion here.

Illustration: Say your loan amount is $115,000 borrowed at 10% interest rate. If this was a 30-year conventional mortgage, your monthly loan payment would be $1,009.21 and you would pay $248,316 in total interest over the term of the loan. On a biweekly mortgage each of your payments would be half of the monthly payment which in this case would be $504.61. But since you're making an equivalent of one extra monthly payment each year, your total interest paid is reduced to $158,193 which is a saving of $90,123 over the 30-year mortgage. Your loan would be paid off in approximately 18 years.

Future of Biweekly Mortgages

Biweekly mortgages do offer a certain advantage over the conventional mortgage. However, they just have not been very popular. Very few mortgage institutions seem to offer such a mortgage. Why?

The main reason for this is the administrative headaches associated with servicing a loan on a biweekly basis. Instead of recording twelve payments each year, a lender is now recording 26 payments. There are more notices to be sent out, more delinquencies to be handled, and more chances for error. For many lenders, the big deterrent has been the prospect of altering their computer software to handle biweekly mortgages. At present, it is estimated that between 150 to 200 lenders offer some sort of biweekly mortgage plan to their borrowers, and most of these lenders are concentrated in the Northeast and, to a lesser extent, in the Midwest.

This situation may, however, change. Starting February 1, 1988, the Federal National Mortgage Association (Fannie Mae) will offer to buy biweekly mortgages just as it has been buying other types of loans and using them to back mortgage securities. The newly formed Biweekly Mortgage Acceptance Corporation (Billie Mae) will also do so.

Fannie Mae, a federally chartered, publicly traded corporation, operates a secondary market for home loans. It purchases residential mortgages from lenders, holding a portion of the loans in its portfolio and repackaging the rest for sale to investors as securities.

These moves are bound to increase the availability of biweekly mortgages, and possibly improve their terms. By some projections, the number of lenders offering biweeklies may soar tenfold to 2,000.

Fannie Mae's entry into the biweekly-mortgage field is expected to broaden the instrument's availability. By providing a ready secondary market for the loans, Fannie Mae would relieve individual lenders of the burden of packaging them for private placement with investors or for sale on Wall Street. And by cutting the lenders' costs of handling such loans, and increasing the competition among lenders offering the loans, Fannie Mae's move should also reduce the interest rates charged on the loans.

Recommendation: If you're looking to obtain a new loan or refinance your present loan, it would behoove to ask around and find a lender that offers you the option of biweekly mortgages. Although you may prepay your loan according to your own schedule as we have described under other plans, the biweekly mortgages offer you a structured prepayment program with few bookkeeping headaches for you.

Adjustable Rate Mortgage

9

Until 1980, there were few adjustable rate mortgages around. In fact, most borrowers hadn't even heard of such mortgages. In 1980 interest rates reached levels nobody thought was possible. Most banks and savings and loan associations were charging 17% on mortgage loans to new homeowners. Such rates made it all but impossible for many a homeowner to qualify for a loan.

The super-high interest rates brought into focus another consideration. Nobody knew how long these interest rates were going to prevail, but most shrewd observers of economy knew that bad times and good times do not stay around for ever. The economy, and the interest rates, go through cycles. In not too distant a future, they surmised, the lower interest rates will return.

And return they did. In fact, as I remember, Home Savings Bank in California dropped their mortgage interest rates over one weekend by five points. If the high interest rate of 17% was abnormal, a drop of this size was equally abnormal. Most mortgages are written for a term of thirty years. The abrupt swings, up or down, in interest rates play havoc with lenders and borrowers alike.

Banks and savings and loan associations, as a rule, like to match as closely as possible their cost of acquiring deposits and return they expect to earn by lending these funds. During these turbulent times, many lenders found themselves with mortgages in their portfolio that were yielding only 6% while the prevailing interest on time deposits in the marketplace was over 14%.

Adjustable rate mortgages were an answer to the lenders' dilemma. But as we'll see in this chapter, what is in the best interest of the lender may or may not be in the best interests of the borrower.

In order to better understand the adjustable rate mortgage, let us first briefly look at fixed rate mortgage and its advantages and disadvantages.

Fixed Rate Mortgage

Just as the name implies, the interest rate on a fixed rate mortgage does not change throughout the life of the mortgage. If you took out an $85,000 mortgage at 9% interest for 30 years, your monthly payments would be pegged at $683.93. No matter whatever happened in the interest rate market, you could sleep peacefully knowing that your mortgage payment would not fluctuate as long as you owned the house.

Advantages and Disadvantages of Fixed Rate Mortgage

First the advantages.

Peace of mind. For a borrower, this is the primary advantage. For most people, home is the biggest investment they'll ever make. Knowing that your biggest investment is not subject to the vagaries of marketplace is a big, big plus.

As the years go by, a fixed rate mortgage takes a smaller bite out of your income. Most people increase their earning capacity over the years. They get raises at work, get promotions, or change to better-paying jobs. With a higher income, the fixed rate mortgage takes a relatively smaller bite out of your monthly budget.

A $700 per month mortgage represents a 28% of a person's income of $2,500. If his income goes up to $3,200, he'll be spending less than 22% of his income on the mortgage. You now have a bigger slice of the pie left to spend on other things.

There's yet one other consideration along these lines. We are living in inflationary times. Not counting true gains in income, inflation has pushed everyone into higher income brackets. What this means is that we're paying back borrowed funds with cheaper dollars. With a fixed rate mortgage, this is a distinct advantage since interest rates have no effect on your payment.

Now the disadvantages.

Fixed rate mortgages are generally not assumable. This is the biggest disadvantage. Except for VA and FHA backed loans, almost all fixed rate mortgages cannot be taken over by the new buyer of the property. You may have a low interest rate loan while everybody else is paying several points higher than you, but when you sell the property, the lender wants you to pay off the loan upon sale. This is known as the "due on sale" clause. The next buyer has to obtain his own mortgage at the then-prevailing interest rates.

If the interest rates decline, you'll not benefit. If you had obtained your fixed rate loan when the interest rates were high and presently they are several points lower, your monthly payments will remain the same. Fluctuations in interest rates market will not affect you one way or the other. If the rates have declined sufficiently, your only recourse would be to refinance the mortgage.

Now let's examine the adjustable rate mortgage and its various novel features.

Adjustable Rate Mortgage

In times of volatile interest rates, such as the period between 1980 and 1984, most savings and loan associations and banks were reluctant to tie up their money for 30 years at a fixed rate, especially since they did not know what the rates were going to be even six months into the future. This was the crucible out of which came the adjustable rate mortgage.

But how do you convince a home buyer to assume the risk of fluctuating interest rates - a risk that has been traditionally borne by lenders?

The lenders began to quote 17 percent interest on fixed rate mortgages, thus effectively shutting a vast majority of first-time buyers out of the market. But at the same time, the lenders were offering adjustable rate mortgages at interest rates of 13 percent. The lenders knew that this new mortgage instrument offered them the security that the fixed rate mortgage did not. If the interest rate in the economy rose, the rate on their ARMs would also rise, and they will be able to keep pace with the market.

The lower interest rate offered with the adjustable rate mortgage was the inducement to potential buyers to assume the risk that the lenders had always traditionally assumed. If a borrower has the choice of getting a fixed rate mortgage or an adjustable rate mortgage at the same rate, he would undoubtedly choose a fixed rate mortgage. If the rate on his fixed-rate mortgage is relatively low, he'll keep the mortgage for as long as he owns the property, and he'll be able to sleep better at night knowing that his payments next month would not rise beyond what he can afford.

Against this backdrop, let's look at the advantages of adjustable rate mortgages.

Availability. As we saw during the years of heady interest rates, many lenders simply refused to write fixed rate mortgages. The only mortgage available was an ARM. This is still true. ARMs are generally easier to find. Lenders are more willing to take risks with them.

Take, for instance, real estate investors. A person who is buying a property for investment purposes is unlikely to find a lender willing to lend him money on a fixed rate mortgage without paying unduly high points. But he can find lenders who'll offer him an ARM at competitive rates.

When fixed rate loans are hard or impossible to find, look for an ARM.

Discount rates. ARMs are not only more readily available, they are also available at a discount. Lenders, in order to attract borrowers to this risky mortgage, offer a lower than normal initial interest rate. If a fixed rate mortgage is offered at 11% interest, you may be able to find an ARM with an initial interest rate of 9%.

This rate is also known as a "teaser rate" because it's good for only a short time, normally six months. After that period, the rate is adjusted to reflect the general market.

Discount rates offered with ARMs make them attractive to another kind of buyer. If you're buying a property with the intention of holding it for only a short period, say one to two years, you'll benefit from the low initial payments. By the time the rate is raised, you'll have sold the property. Some investors go for an ARM with this idea in mind. It minimizes their cash outlay during the short period of investment.

Illustration: A buyer of a home in 1984 had a choice of accepting a fixed rate mortgage at 13 percent interest or an adjustable mortgage at 9 percent introductory rate. This introductory rate could rise a maximum of 2 percent annually. The "margin" on the loan was 2.5 percent which meant that after the first six months the interest rate was going to be computed by adding 2.5% to the index stipulated in the loan agreement. In this case, it meant that the new rate after six months became 11.5 percent. If the investor intends to hold the property for only eighteen months to two years, he would actually save money by going with the adjustable rate mortgage.

ARMs: Easier to qualify for. ARMs have caught on with the general public partly because they are easier to qualify for. This may be a deceptive benefit, but for a new homeowner it could make the difference between owning a home or not owning one. Since the lenders determine a buyer's qualifications on the basis of the initial mortgage payment which, in turn, is kept artificially low by "teaser" rates, many homeowners who cannot possibly qualify for a fixed-rate mortgage find it easier to qualify for an ARM.

Illustration: A borrower obtaining an ARM of $130,000 at 8.75% faces monthly mortgage payments of $1,022.72. If he were to opt for a fixed rate mortgage at 10%, he'll be paying $1,140.85 per month. In terms of income required to qualify, he'll need nearly 15% higher income to qualify for the fixed rate mortgage. This often spells the difference between owning the home or not.

Caution: The fact that the lender does not qualify you on the basis of actual monthly payments you'll be making after the initial introductory period does not mean that you should also ignore the hard reality. Keep in mind that after the first six months you'll be paying substantially higher payments. If you have not foreseen this certainty and provided for in your budget, you're asking for trouble.

Assumability. This often is cited as an advantage of an ARM. In many cases, this is true. Even though the new buyer will be assuming a loan that is adjusted every six months to reflect the changes in the interest rate market, he'll generally find it easier to qualify for an existing loan. As a rule, the costs involved in assuming a loan are somewhat lower than in obtaining a similar new loan.

A seller of a home can use this feature effectively to market his property to prospective buyers.

Declining interest rates benefit ARMs. This is one other important advantage of ARMs. When the interest rate goes down, the rate on the ARM also goes down. In a fixed rate loan, you're stuck with whatever interest rate you had started out with.

As a counter argument, one may point out that when the interest rates decline, one can refinance a fixed rate mortgage to take advantage of the lower interest. This is easier said than done.

Refinancing has its high attendant costs in the form of loan origination fees and other closing costs. As a rule of thumb, there has to be a drop of at least two percent points in interest rate from your existing mortgage to make it economically feasible to refinance your property. If the rate declines by only about a half point, it will not make economic sense to refinance your mortgage. On the other hand, an ARM will benefit from every little drop in interest rate without further costs.

ARM Features

Most borrowers find ARMs much more difficult to understand compared to fixed rate mortgages. They have many features that often are not fully explained by loan officers.

In the next chapter, we'll briefly discuss some of these features.

More on ARMs 10

This is the feature that distinguishes ARMs from fixed rate mortgages. All ARMs are indexed. They move in tandem with some well-recognized index that measures the current cost of money. If this index goes up, the interest on your ARM will go up. If the followed index goes down, your interest rate (and your monthly payment) will go down correspondingly.

Most Commonly Used Indices

Here are some of the most commonly used indices.

1. **Six-month T-bill yields**

2. **One-year T-bill yields**

3. **Three-year T-bill yields**

4. **Monthly weighted average cost of funds (generally for the Eleventh District savings institutions)**

5. **Cost of fixed-rate mortgages over a long term**

A bank or a savings and loan association is not required to use a particular index. The regulatory agencies, the Office of the Comptroller of the Currency in the case of banks and the Federal

Home Loan Bank Board in the case of savings and loan associations, do, however, require that the mortgage institution choose an
index over which it has no control, is widely published, and
reflects the interest rates in general.

More commonly used indices are the six-month T-bill
yields and the cost of funds for the Federal Home Loan Bank
Board. For instance, California Federal Savings and Loan Asso-
ciation uses the monthly weighted average cost of funds for the
Eleventh District as computed monthly by the Federal Home
Loan Bank of San Francisco.

Volatility of the Index

Most ARMs make rate and payment adjustments once
every six months or a year. So the determining factor in evaluating
a particular ARM would be the movement of the index in the past
six to twelve months. In choosing an ARM, you must look for a
bank or savings and loan association that follows an index that is
fairly stable. Some indices are more volatile than others. Slight
changes in the general economic situation or interest rate market
may produce a more pronounced fluctuation in certain indices.
Some others may remain stable through minor peaks and valleys
in interest rates.

With a volatile index, your monthly payments on each
adjustment date may suffer a sharp rise or fall. With a more stable
index, the ripple effect of the changes in the interest rate market
will take relatively longer to affect you.

Illustration: Cost of funds for FHLBB is generally considered to
be a more stable index than the six-month T-bill yields. During
1985 and 1986, the interest rates in general were dropping but the

index based on the cost of funds for FHLBB did not show any appreciable downward movement. The homeowners whose ARMs were based on this index continued to pay higher payments while they were reading daily in the newspapers the continual drop in the interest rate market. On the other hand, when the interest rates do go up, these same homeowners are not likely to see a sudden jump in their monthly payments.

The six-month yield on Treasury securities reflects more sharply and immediately any changes in the general interest market. Loans tied to this index are more likely to drop when interest rates decline, and rise equally sharply when the rates go up.

That is why when comparing ARMs, it is vital to consider the index. The two most common indices are the monthly 11th District Cost of Funds index and the one-year "constant maturity" treasury rates (T-bills).

Comparison Between Two Indices

The 11th District Cost of Funds index is the weighted average cost of all funds that flow into the 239 savings institutions in California, Arizona and Nevada. The sources used to calculate the weighted average cost of funds include savings accounts, checking accounts, Federal Home Loan Bank advances, money market accounts, certificates of deposit and other borrowed money.

Because the weighted average cost of funds also includes long-term accounts, the index is more stable than other indices.

The other popular index is tied to one-year "constant maturity" treasury rates (T-bills). The index is the U.S. Treasury's estimate of the yield on all outstanding treasury securities with a remaining life of one year (the original terms may have been longer).

Historically, the 11th District Cost of Funds index has been the most stable of indices to which ARMs are tied. For example, in 1981, the Federal Reserve prime rate reached almost 21%, and the one-year T-bill rate exceeded 16%, yet the highest the 11th District Cost of Funds index ever reached was 12.673% in 1982, and that was for one month only.

Comparison of savings between the one-year T-bill index and the monthly 11th District Cost of Funds index further emphasizes the advantages of the latter.

If two borrowers had identical $100,000 ARMs - one tied to the 11th District Cost of Funds index, the other to the one-year T-bill - the borrower with the ARM tied to the Cost of Funds index would have saved $120.44 more per month from 1979 to mid-year 1985. That represents a total savings of nearly $8,000 during this 66-month period.

In times of declining interest rates the one-year T-bill will fall more rapidly than the Cost of Funds index because it is more volatile. However, when interest rates rise rapidly, the one-year T-Bill has a history of rising faster - and to much higher levels - than the 11th District Cost of Funds.

Moreover, ARMs based on the 11th District Cost of Funds index carry an annual cap of 7.5% on payment increases, while many Treasury-based ARMs carry an annual interest rate cap of two percentage points. Thus, a borrower who took out a 9%

Treasury-based ARM for $100,000 could face an 11% rate in one year, representing a 22% increase in monthly payments.

ARM Indices Compared

(In percent)

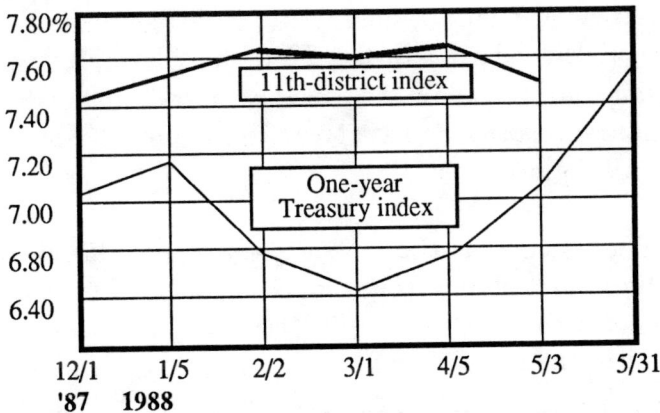

NOTE: The one-year Treasury index is an adjusted weekly average yield on U.S. Treasury securities. The 11th district index is a monthly weighted average cost of funds to members of the 11th Federal Home Loan Bank Board district.

Source: Federal National Mortgage Association

Convertible ARM

Another alternative is simply converting to a fixed-rate loan, eliminating interest rate risk altogether.

Consumers can now buy ARMs with a convertibility feature. Homeowners with such loans can elect to switch to a fixed rate, usually after the mortgage's first year, and before its fifth, but at a cost. These mortgages typically carry a higher interest rate of from one-half to three-quarters of a percentage point, plus an average lenders' fee of $250 and one-half to one percent of the loan balance.

Even for homeowners who are stuck with a volatile ARM without a convertibility feature, it is still relatively inexpensive to convert to either a cost-of-funds ARM or a fixed loan. Most lenders will demand a fee equal to 2% of the balance of the loan, but bargains are available as thrifts and banks try to invest the $89 billion of new deposits that have poured into their vaults since the October 1987 crash.

For instance, Home Savings of America, the nation's largest thrift and a unit of H.F. Ahmanson & Co., Los Angeles, currently offers a cost-of-funds ARM at 9.4%, plus a one-time fee of half a percentage point on the loan's balance outstanding and $250. Goldome Realty Credit Corp., a unit of Buffalo, N.Y.-based Goldome bank, will refinance ARMs into fixed-rate loans for no points, for current customers.

Mortgage borrowers should compare the cost of conversion to their assessment of the risk from rising rates. For example, a Treasury-indexed, $100,000 ARM at 9.5% would face an increase of $150 a month, or $1,800 a year, if the rate jumped to 11.5%. That borrower could convert to, say, a 9.4% cost-of-funds ARM or a 30-year fixed loan at 10.5% for fees and escrow costs of about $2,250, assuming a loan-origination charge of one-half percentage point.

This $2,250 amount would be recouped in 30 months under the 10.5% fixed rate mortgage, compared with the ARM at 11.5%. As for the 9.4% cost-of-funds ARM, it would be more than $1,000 cheaper over a one-year period compared with the

11.5% Treasury-based ARM.

Recommendation: If you plan to keep your mortgage a long time, choose an index that is most stable. If you plan to keep the mortgage for only a short time, consider an index that is currently the lowest.

Margin

In an adjustable rate mortgage, the interest on your loan fluctuates in correspondence with one of the predetermined indices. However, the rate you pay isn't the same as the rate of the index. For example, if the yield on six-month T-bills is the index used and their interest rate happens to be 7%, the rate charged on your ARM will not be 7%. The lender will add a "margin" to this rate to arrive at your interest rate.

Margin is the number of points added to the index to arrive at your interest rate. Generally, this ranges from 1 to 3 points and does not change over the life of the loan. Margin is added to an index so that the interest rate charged on your loan is in conformity with the general interest rates prevailing in the mortgage market. Obviously, in seeking an ARM, you should look for the lowest possible margin.

Index rate + Margin = ARM interest rate

Adjustment Period

Each ARM specifies the frequency with which it will adjust the interest rate. The lender will select this period in most cases, but often you may be able to negotiate this feature on your loan. Again, what you're looking for is a relatively longer interval between each adjustment.

In some mortgages, the interest rate is adjusted each month based on the index chosen by the lender, but the payments may change only annually. Then, there are some other mortgages in which the rate and the payments change every six months. If the lender is following a one-year T-bill yield, the adjustment period probably will be yearly. If, on the other hand, it is following a six-month T-bill yield, the adjustment period will be six months. There are innumerable variations, and each lending institution follows its own policies.

Recommendation: Go for an adjustment period of either six months or one year. Monthly adjustments produce too much volatility and uncertainty. Anything longer than one year, and you'll not be able to benefit from the decline in interest rates and will have to make a large adjustment when it becomes due.

Interest Rate Cap

Every borrower looking at an adjustable rate mortgage is haunted by the fear of runaway interest rates. As we saw a few years back, interest rates of 17% all but devastated the real estate market in America. A vast majority of people could simply not afford those sky-high interest rates. Sellers were sitting on their properties for months on end with nay an offer.

But what if you had signed up for an adjustable rate mortgage at 10% and then the interest rate shot up to 17%? You probably would not be able to keep up with the monthly payments and may face the prospect of losing your home. Just to allay these fears, and to make ARMs slightly more palatable to the skeptical borrowers, the mortgage lending institutions came up with the idea of interest rate cap.

Almost all ARMs have an interest rate cap, generally of five percent points. Your interest rate during the life of the mortgage cannot go up or down more than five points from the initial rate. If your initial rate is 10%, the worst rate you may face would be 15%. By the same token, the lowest mortgage interest you would ever pay would be 5%.

Illustration: You have a mortgage of $100,000 with an initial interest rate of 10%. The ARM contract calls for an interest rate cap of 5%. Here is what will happen in the best and worst case scenario:

	Interest Rate	Monthly Payment
Original interest rate	10%	$ 878
Maximum interest rate	15%	1,264
Minimum interest rate	5%	492

If you think you can live with the maximum possible interest rate and the monthly payment, you've nothing to fear. If you cannot, you must make allowance for those possible bad times.

Caution: Be sure that the interest rate cap on your ARM applies to the introductory rate, say 8%, and not to the adjusted rate which would be index plus the lender's margin, which could be 10% to 11%.

Interest Rate Steps

Say an ARM allows for an interest rate cap of 5%. The initial interest rate was 10%. When the next adjustment period comes due, the movement in the index calls for a raise in your mortgage interest rate of 4%. Could your interest rate be hiked to 14% in one single step? With most ARMs presently being written, this is not likely.

For practical purposes, more than the interest rate cap, it's important to ensure that your monthly payments do not jump an inordinate amount in any single adjustment period. "Steps" refer to the amount by which the mortgage interest rate can be increased (or decreased) each adjustment period.

Nearly all ARMs have steps, or limits on the increase in the interest rate allowed per adjustment period. In any one period, the interest rate is generally not allowed to rise more than a point or two. For example, California Federal Savings ARM specifies a maximum increase or decrease of 1% each adjustment period, 2% annually, and 5% over the life of the loan. Such additional limits provide you with a little more stability and predictability in your mortgage.

Interest rates typically fluctuate up or down; they don't just go up and stay up or go down and stay down. So when the interest rate has shot up suddenly, if your mortgage calls for a smaller step increase, say 1% against 2% per adjustment period, the blow to your monthly budget as a result of higher mortgage payments will be spread over at least two adjustment periods. By the time your mortgage has made the full adjustment, the interest rates may have started their downward journey.

Recommendation: Look for smaller step increases in your mortgage; you'll have a more stable mortgage.

Monthly Payment Caps

More than the changes in the interest rates, most borrowers are concerned with the size of their monthly mortgage payments. They want to make sure that they can afford any changes in the monthly payment from one adjustment period to the next. Many ARMs have this feature. They allow that the payment from one period to the next may not change more than a certain percent, say 7.5%, of the previous amount.

Some ARMs place limits on the interest rate fluctuation, but place no limit on monthly payments. Some others place a limit on the interest rate as well as monthly payments.

Illustration: Let's take the same 30-year, $100,000 mortgage at 10% and look at the effect of the payment cap. Interest rate in this example fluctuates from 10% to 12%.

	Previous Period	New Period
Interest rate	10%	12%
Payment without monthly cap	$878	$1,029
Payment with 7.5% cap	$878	$944
Difference		$85

The cap on the increase allowed per adjustment period in your monthly mortgage payment would, in this example, save you $85 per month. But here is the bad news. The $85 a month saved is simply added to the mortgage balance, which means that the amount you owe your lender actually increases over time. This is referred to as "negative amortization."

Many lenders have a policy of "recasting" the loan after, say, five years to take care of the negative amortization. Based on the new outstanding balance, the loan payments are increased to fully amortize the loan over its original term.

So, as a rule, the monthly payment cap may mean lower payments now, but may result in higher payments later.

To soften the impact of negative amortization somewhat, most mortgages contain both a monthly payment cap and an interest rate cap. Such a loan may appear on the surface better than one with just the interest rate cap. But in reality this isn't so. When a mortgage has both an interest rate and monthly payment cap, the interest rate cap is set higher than the monthly payment cap which still results in negative amortization. If the interest rate cap were set sufficiently low so that no negative amortization occurs, there would be no need for the monthly payment cap.

Are Adjustable Rate Mortgages Making a Comeback?

Adjustable rate mortgages made their first splash in the real estate market in early 1980s. For a time, ARMs were the only game in town for many mortgage institutions. They continued to replace the fixed rate mortgages for a long time until in 1986 their market share peaked at 65% of all home loans. As the interest rates continued their steady decline, the fixed rate mortgages recaptured a part of the lost market share. In 1987, the ARMs dipped to 21% in terms of the home loan mortgage market, but since then their market share has climbed back to 31%.

There are two main reasons for the comeback that the ARMs appear to be staging.

● **The gap between adjustable and fixed rates is widening again.** There is a general feeling among lenders that interest rates have fallen as far as they are ever going to fall. Lenders would like the borrowers to shoulder the risk of any future rate increases. Therefore, they have attempted to make the ARMs more attractive by lowering the initial interest rate they offer on these mortgages. Many homeowners find these rates a once-in-a-lifetime bargain and they're snapping up ARMs at an increased pace.

● **First time home buyers and those trading up to more expensive homes find ARMs particularly attractive.** The low introductory rates offered on ARMs have made it possible for many new home buyers to qualify for loans that they didn't think was possible until now. There is also increased optimism in the real estate market that the pace of appreciation in properties will enable them to sell their existing homes in a short time and move on to more expensive homes. Appreciation in the home price, they hope, will more than offset any negative amortization that an ARM may cause.

How the home-loan market breaks down between adjustable and fixed-rate mortgages

YEAR	ADJUSTABLE-RATE LOANS	FIXED-RATE LOANS
1983	28%	72%
1984	52%	48%
1985	41%	59%
1986	25%	75%
1987	36%	64%
April 1988	48%	52%

Source: Mortgage Bankers Association

Graduated
Payment Mortgage 11

Introduction

Generally speaking, home buyers can be classified into two major categories. First, there is a buyer who already owns a home but wishes to move into a higher-priced, better-situated home. He may also be relocating due to a job transfer. In fact, well over 85% of home purchases in this country are made by people who already own a home. For this class of home buyers circumstances are a little different. They may have built up an equity in their previous home over the years and they are in a position to cash in this equity by selling the home and use the proceeds as a down payment on the next home. These home buyers as a rule are older, have had several years of work experience, and are usually moving into their second, or third homes. By having built up an equity in their homes they are able to convert that equity into a sizable down payment and consequently incur a smaller monthly mortgage payment on the new home.

The second class of home buyers consists of people who are just entering the work force, or may have been saving money over the years to buy their first home. For these people coming up with a down payment sufficient to satisfy the lenders' requirement is a major task. But more critically, they are limited in the size of the mortgage that they can qualify for due to the lower income. They haven't quite reached the peak of their productive career.

They may have the expectations of earning higher income over the next few years. However, at the present time they have to find an innovative source of financing that will enable them to break into the home market.

Graduated Payment Mortgage

The answer to their dilemma lies in the unique form of mortgage, called graduated payment mortgage (GPM). Graduated payment mortgage allows them to qualify for a home now - years sooner than they would be able to under conventional financing methods. Looking at it from another angle, the same level of income allows them to qualify for a more expensive home than otherwise possible. In return for this early qualification, they expect to pay a gradually increasing monthly mortgage over the next few years.

Graduated payment mortgages are designed for people with rising incomes. They feature fixed interest rates plus low initial monthly payments that allow a home buyer to get into a home that he can afford with the payments rising annually during the first years of the loan. As the borrower's income rises, the monthly payments rise too. The monthly mortgage payments toward the end of the loan are large enough to amortize the loan completely in the same number of years as a conventional loan.

Illustration: Let's take as an example a couple that is in the process of buying their first home. Their combined annual income is $24,300. If 28% of their income can be devoted to the payment of mortgage interest and principal as most lenders would require, they can pay up to $566.98 a month as mortgage payment. At 10%

interest over 30 years this monthly payment of $566.98 translates into a maximum mortgage of $64,607.84. However, with a graduated payment mortgage plan, they can afford a house with a mortgage of $85,000.

The monthly mortgage payment under the graduated payment mortgage plan would be lower than that for a constantly amortizing conventional mortgage. According to one plan, their monthly payment would rise 7 1/2% annually for the first five years of the loan. From years 6 thru 30, the payment would rise to the level of $813.98 and would remain there throughout the duration of the loan. Compare this monthly payment to the payment required under the conventional constantly amortizing loan of the same amount, the payment being $745.94.

The table shown below shows the difference between a graduated payment mortgage and a conventional mortgage. In the first year of the loan the borrower is paying only $566.98 whereas he would have had to pay $745.94 under the conventional mortgage program. For a first-time home buyer the difference between these two amounts may mean the difference between owning a home or not. In fact, as you look at the figures the borrowers are paying almost 24% less under the graduated payment plan in the first year.

Assuming the couple's income rises every year, at least to the tune of 7 1/2%, they will be able to meet their mortgage obligations comfortably. Looking at the schedule shown in the table, it is obvious that due to the low monthly payments paid during the first five years of the loan, the loan is bound to produce negative amortization. In order to fully pay off the loan in 30 years, it is necessary that the payments be greater in the last 25 years of the loan. In other words, the borrowers would be paying

$813.98 for the balance of the term of 25 years, as against $745.94 under a conventional loan program.

GPM versus Conventional Financing

	GPM*	Conventional
Loan Size	$85,000	$85,000
Loan Term	30 years	30 years
Interest rate	10 percent	10 percent
Monthly payment		
Year 1	$ 566.98	$ 745.94
Year 2	609.50	745.94
Year 3	655.21	745.94
Year 4	704.36	745.94
Year 5	757.19	745.94
Year 6-30	813.98	745.94
Year-end loan balance		
Year 1	$86,776.13	$84,527.50
Year 2	88,204.00	84,005.53
Year 3	89,206.98	83,428.90
Year 4	89,697.42	82,791.89
Year 5	89,575.40	82,088.17
Year 6	88,727.00	81,310.77
Year 7	87,789.75	80,451.96
Year 8	86,754.36	79,503.23
Year 30	-	-
Yearly negative amortization		
Year 1	$ 1,776.13	-
Year 2	1,427.87	-
Year 3	1,002.98	-
Year 4	490.44	-

Year 5	122.02	-
Year 6	-	-

---

*GPM loan with 7.5 percent payment increase annually for five years.

SOURCE: GPM figures based on HUD Transmittal Document No. 4, Appendix 1, Page 3 (Jan. 21, 1978).

Types of Graduated Payment Mortgages

Graduated payment mortgages are offered by most conventional lenders, like banks and savings and loan associations. In addition to these traditional sources, financing is also available under the FHA Section 245 for owner-occupied single family homes and condominiums. There are at least five different kinds of plans available under FHA/HUD plan.

We'll briefly summarize these plans here for you.

Plan 1: Under this plan monthly payments rise at 2 1/2 percent each year during the first five years of the loan. Generally speaking, this plan does not produce substantial savings during the graduated payment life of the mortgage. It does not produce sufficient savings in the first year of the loan to make it attractive for many home buyers. It may be sufficient for someone who is just trying to squeeze into a new home.

Plan 2: Under this plan monthly payments increase 5% each year during the first five years of the loan. Here the savings in the first and second year of the loan are substantial enough to make the graduated payment mortgage attractive for a home buyer.

Plan 3: This plan carries the above process of increasing the monthly payments further; the payments increase 7 1/2% each year during the first five years of the loan. The percent savings in the first year over conventional financing here is about 25%. This plan is probably the most attractive of all the plans described so far. The first year payments under this plan being as low as 25% and gradually rising over the next four years make the plan most suitable for many new home buyers. They also figure that by year 5, their income would have risen significantly where they can afford to make the higher monthly payments. Some buyers also figure on selling their property after 5 years. If they do so, they would have enjoyed in the meantime the fruits of lower monthly payments.

There are two more plans.

Plan 4: Under this plan, monthly payments increase two percent each year during the first ten years of the loan. This is not an attractive proposition from a borrower's standpoint. By stretching the graduated payment schedule over a period of ten years, he, in fact, is increasing his interest costs significantly over the life of the loan. Similar to extending the life of a mortgage, extending the life of the graduated payment mortgage does not produce significantly lower monthly payments, but it does raise the cost of borrowing money over the term of the loan.

Plan 5: This plan takes the above program one step further with monthly payments increasing 3% each year during the first 10 years of the loan.

Combining the GPM with the ARM

With the advent of adjustable rate mortgages it is now possible to combine the benefit of low initial monthly payments of a graduated payment mortgage with an adjustable rate mortgage. With this plan the borrower typically gets very low initial payments for a set period of time. Since payments are fixed but the interest rate is not, it is possible that negative amortization will occur in the first years of the loan. At the conclusion of the initial period when monthly payments are set, a graduated payment adjustable rate mortgage would behave just like a regular adjustable rate mortgage with payments and interest rates that could vary throughout the life of the loan.

A typical GPARM loan will have a graduated payment period of between three and ten years with five years being the most common. In other words, after five years the payments will be raised to the level that would allow the loan to be fully amortized. The monthly payments during the first five years of the loan would typically rise at 7 1/2%.

A GPARM is probably a better financing instrument than a simple ARM, especially for young home buyers. The borrower has the advantage of knowing in advance exactly how much the payment is going to increase each period during the graduation time. Under a straight adjustable rate mortgage the borrower has no way of knowing what his next adjustment period is going to bring.

The biggest disadvantage of the ARM/GPM is negative amortization. This occurs because the payment schedule is set up so that the monthly payment does not cover the full amount of the interest. The unpaid interest accumulates and is added to the principal mortgage amount. As with all loans that feature negative amortizations, after having made payments for the first 5 years, you may end up owing more than you had borrowed originally. If you intend to move in less than 5 years you may find that the sale price does not cover the outstanding mortgage. Unless the house has appreciated over these years you may find yourself in a difficult predicament. After paying sales commissions and closing costs you may find that you cannot even get your down payment back from the sales proceeds. In fact, it's not inconceivable that after 3 or 5 years it might cost you money out of your pocket just to sell the property. This is a big danger of a graduated payment mortgage. If you decide to go for this mortgage you want to be sure that the house you're buying is in an area of high demand and rapid appreciation, or you may have to resign yourself to living in the house for a long time.

Graduated payment mortgages are available not only under FHA/HUD program plans, but also from other private lenders including both banks and savings and loan associations. Although these financial institutions may be authorized to offer GPMs many do not. Many lenders find GPMs simply too difficult and too risky. They are afraid that borrowers may not be able to afford higher payments necessitated after the first 5 years and that they may have to foreclose on the property which has already accrued negative amortization. Therefore, in order to find a GPM, with or without an adjustable rate mortgage, you may have to look around hard. Federally chartered savings and loans and mortgage bankers are probably your best bet.

Who should go for a GPM?

As we have said before, a graduated payment mortgage is almost a necessity for many first-time home buyers. For them, in order to be able to afford a house, a graduated payment mortgage is about the only source of financing since they cannot afford the higher payments required under the conventional mortgage. Without a GPM they would be forced to continue to rent.

Typically, a GPM works best for a young couple or an individual in the 25-35 age group. For this group advancement and general salary increases are normal either in their career or through switching of jobs. By the same token, a graduated payment mortgage is not a device suitable for individuals with fixed income.

A graduated payment mortgage not only reduces your monthly payment making it possible for you to qualify for a mortgage, but it also allows you to qualify for a higher mortgage than otherwise possible. Just to give you an idea, if you can afford to pay $1,100 in monthly mortgage payments, you'll be able to afford a mortgage worth $125,000 at 10% interest over a 30-year loan term. With a graduated payment mortgage, the same monthly payment would allow you to look for a property that would support a mortgage of over $155,000. A GPM allows you to keep a monthly payment within your budget and also allows you to buy a higher priced home than you would otherwise be able to afford.

FHA and VA Mortgages

12

During the 1950s and 1960s most Americans looked to FHA and VA as their primary source for mortgage. These were the most popular mortgages. They offered attractive financing and easy qualifying. However, as the real estate prices soared, FHA and VA did not keep pace with the market place, and home buyers turned to private lenders. Recently, these mortgages have made a comeback and they still are the bast bargain if you can obtain one.

In this chapter, we'll examine various requirements and advantages of FHA and VA loans. Keep in mind that for various reasons you may not be able to qualify for either of these loans and you may have to resort to a bank or savings and loan association as your source for mortgage money.

FHA Mortgages

Technically speaking, Federal Housing Authority (FHA) does not lend money to borrowers. Instead, it insures mortgages. A borrower works with his local bank or an S&L to obtain the mortgage, and if it is an FHA loan, the federal governmental agency will insure the mortgage. In the event of a default of the borrower, FHA will pay off the lender.

Here are the advantages of an FHA backed mortgage.

Advantages of FHA Mortgage

1. An FHA mortgage is fully assumable. This is the biggest advantage. You can pass on your FHA loan to the buyer of your property. In these times of volatile interest rates, if your loan was obtained at a low interest rate, it's easy to attract prospective buyers to your property with an assumable loan.

2. There are no prepayment penalties. An FHA loan cannot have a prepayment penalty.

3. FHA requires that the buyer and the property qualify for the loan. FHA has established certain standards for the property. If the property does not meet these specifications, the seller has to bring the property up to the FHA standard. It is a comforting thought that the home you're buying meets the federal standards set for housing.

Now here are the requirements of an FHA mortgage which may also be looked upon as its disadvantages.

Requirements of the FHA Mortgage

1. Currently, maximum FHA loan amount is $90,000. Inflation in the real estate market has pushed up the housing prices considerably higher than this amount. In California or the Northeast, you'll be hard pressed to find a home that meets this loan amount. Effectively, this limit on the loan amount shuts out a vast majority of areas for a home buyer looking at an FHA mortgage.

2. Under FHA terms, an owner-occupied property qualifies for 5 percent down payment. For an investor, the down payment has to be a minimum of 15 percent.

3. FHA requires a borrower to pay mortgage insurance premium. This adds extra cost to the loan. On a loan of $90,000, you'll pay $3,420 in insurance premium.

VA Mortgages

VA program is another program administered by the federal government to make affordable mortgages available to veterans. Needless to say, you have to be a veteran to obtain a VA mortgage.

The biggest advantage of a VA loan is that you can buy a house without any down payment (with the exception of closing costs.) VA requires you to occupy the home. But, just as an FHA mortgage, a VA loan is fully assumable by the next buyer of the property.

With a VA loan, you work with your local bank or savings and loan association. Veterans Administration guarantees $27,500 of the loan. In the event of a default of the borrower, VA will pay the lender first $27,500 of the loan.

Down Payment

As of this writing, these are the maximum VA mortgages:

Maximum loan amount with no down: $110,000
"Little down," maximum loan amount: $135,000

The "little down" program works like this. The veteran receives a no-down mortgage up to $110,000. If the property costs more, however, the veteran can then put down 25 percent of the amount of $110,000 and the loan will handle the other 75 percent up to a total loan value of $135,000.

Impound Accounts

Both FHA and VA mortgages require you to establish an impound account for your property taxes and insurance. Your monthly payment would therefore be for principal, interest, taxes and insurance.

Refund on an FHA Mortgage

If you had bought your home on an FHA mortgage and had paid it off, you may now be entitled to a substantial cash refund. The Federal Housing Administration requires a homeowner to pay insurance premiums to protect the mortgage lenders against defaults. These premiums are collected in special funds. When the economy is healthy and there are fewer defaults this fund ends up with surpluses. Any surpluses that are remaining in the fund are by law required to be distributed to the homeowners when they pay off the mortgage.

This is how the system is supposed to work. However, often the refund doesn't get paid to the homeowner who has paid off his mortgage. This may happen when a lender fails to notify FHA that the loan has been paid off. It can also happen if the original borrower has moved out of his home and cannot be located.

In such cases, unpaid refunds are accumulated by the FHA, broken down by each state until the money is paid back to the homeowners. Just to give you an example, a recent survey of FHA records for Washington, D.C. area showed that people who had borrowed money under the FHA programs were owed refunds anywhere from a hundred dollars to almost two thousand dollars.

In order to collect these refunds, the homeowner must have been paying the mortgage at the time it was paid off and must have been doing so for the preceding 90 days. If the homeowner has moved out of the home and has passed on the FHA mortgage to a new homebuyer, the refund would belong to the person who has assumed the mortgage from you. There is one additional requirement. The mortgage must also have been in existence for at least seven years.

You may satisfy all of these requirements and still not be entitled to a refund if the area that you live in has experienced a high rate of foreclosures so that there is no money to pass out. In other words, the pool where the premium money is collected has been exhausted to pay off the defaults that have occurred in that particular area.

If you think that you are entitled to a refund and you want to inquire further, you should call the FHA Service Center in Washington, D.C., telephone number (202) 755-5616. You must also have your FHA case number handy. This is a 9-digit number that appears on appraisal documents or the mortgage instrument itself.

Reverse Annuity Mortgage 13

In their continuing quest to expand the mortgage market by offering exotic products, many lenders came up with the concept of reverse annuity mortgages in the late 1970s. These mortgages were designed to satisfy a specific demand in the market, especially elderly homeowners who either own their homes free and clear of any debt or owe very little on them. Although they may have built up a large equity in their homes through rapid appreciation in real estate prices, many of these homeowners face the dilemma of limited cash flow to meet their day-to-day needs. If only they could unlock the equity in their home and turn it into a steady stream of cash - such is what the dreams of marketing executives are made of.

How a Reverse Annuity Mortgage Works

Here's how a reverse annuity mortgage works. A lending institution makes the homeowner a loan for up to 80% of its appraised value, typically for 5, 10 or 12 years. The institution, which takes its loan fees and points on the full amount when the loan is approved, then pays the homeowner the balance of the loan in equal monthly installments - minus accruing interest on the already disbursed funds - for the remaining term. The loan - actually the amount disbursed plus interest - can be repaid early if the house is sold by the owner or his heirs. Otherwise, the homeowner is liable to repay the full amount when the loan term expires or he'll face foreclosure.

Here's a real-life example. The homeowners, a San Francisco Bay Area couple, qualified for a $150,000 loan at 10.5% interest in 1987. They paid a total of $3,450 in loan fees and closing costs from the loan proceeds and are receiving $430.51 each month for 10 years. If the loan is not repaid earlier, the couple is responsible for repaying the full $150,000 to the bank in 1997.

Example: Assume that a husband and wife, both sixty-five years old, own their $58,000 home free and clear, and that they obtain a 10-year rising-debt reverse annuity mortgage for $45,000 at 9 percent interest rate. The lender would send them a check for $226.45 per month for ten years. At the end of ten years, the couple would have received a total of $27,173.40, and would owe the lender a total of $45,000. The interest owed to the lender would be $17,826.57, or $148.55 per month for the 10-year period.

Assuming that the home did not change in value during the ten-year period, the remaining equity in the $58,000 RAM example would be $13,000. At this point, the couple could sell the home, pay off the lender, and retain the remaining $13,000 equity. If the couple passed away before the end of the ten-year period, the proceeds of the estate would be used to repay the outstanding balance of the loan. In either case, the couple would have lived in the home while simultaneously reducing their equity.

Combining with Annuity

Another version of the RAM combines a rising-debt loan with a deferred life-annuity policy purchased from a life insurance company. A partial disbursement of the loan proceeds would purchase the annuity, deferring lifetime payments to the annuitant to some future date. The balance of the loan is paid monthly to the borrower until the annuity payments from the life insurance company begin. This modification of a rising-debt RAM defers payment of the loan until estate settlement, protecting the borrower against principal repayment of the loan until death while shifting the time-uncertain annuity payments to the life insurance company.

Is Reverse Annuity Mortgage For You?

It is obvious from the very nature of a reverse annuity mortgage that this option is not for everyone. A homeowner who takes out a reverse annuity mortgage in essence is selling a portion of his home every month. If he outlives the term of the mortgage he is faced with the choice of selling his home to pay off the mortgage. Therefore, the only people who might want to get into such a mortgage are those who do not expect to outlive the term of the mortgage. For an elderly homeowner a reverse annuity mortgage provides a source of much-needed cash to meet his living expenses in the waning days of his life. It definitely is not an option for someone who is healthy and has a long life expectancy.

Precisely for these reasons, many banks and mortgage lenders do not want to get involved with reverse annuity mortgages. No bank is going to risk the public relations debacle by trying to evict an elderly couple from their home or forcing them to sell their home because they have outlived the term of their reverse annuity mortgage. Even the few lenders who do offer such a mortgage require the prospective borrowers to seek counseling and legal advice before incurring such an undertaking.

Private Mortgage Insurance
14

Most first-time home buyers, as a rule, are looking to put as little down as possible, borrowing the rest from a lender. A typical buyer may have scraped just enough money together to put 5% of the purchase price as down payment. Most lenders, however, require a minimum of 10% down payment on a home. In some cases this requirement may even go up to 20%. For example, where an investor is looking to buy a property as a non-owner occupied property he may be required to put 15-20% of the purchase price down.

Is there a way around this onerous requirement?

PMI May Be the Solution

One way a borrower can reduce his down payment is by acquiring private mortgage insurance. A private mortgage insurance (PMI) is designed to make good on a loan in the event of a default by the borrower. It works similar to an FHA insurance. The private insurance company insures the lender against loss for the top 20 - 25% of the mortgage.

Illustration: For example, on a mortgage of $100,000 a PMI of 25% would mean that the lender would be compensated up to $25,000 in the event of a default by the borrower. If a borrower defaults, the lender would foreclose on the property and repossess it. Since the lender is not in the business of owning real estate, he would put up the property for sale and attempt to recoup as much of the investment as possible. Let us say that the property sells for $75,000 on the market. The private mortgage insurance company would reimburse the lender for $25,000 who will suffer no loss as a result of the borrower's default. If the sale of the property brings less than $75,000, the lender would lose because the PMI would pay only up to $25,000.

The private mortgage insurance company insures the mortgage by charging a fee. The fee varies from 1/4 to 1/2% of an interest rate. This amount is added to the mortgage payment and is paid by the borrower. For instance, if the mortgage interest rate is 10%, with PMI the rate would be 10 1/4%. A borrower would be willing to pay this extra 1/4 point interest in return for the lower down payment. He could obtain a 95% loan with private mortgage insurance whereas, without it, he would have to come up with 10% or more as down payment.

Qualifying for PMI

A borrower has to qualify for PMI just as he has to qualify for a loan with the lender. He has to meet not only the lender's but the insurer's requirements as well. Generally speaking, a PMI company imposes more stringent qualifying standards. Where a lender might be willing to qualify you with a monthly mortgage payment that could be as much as 30% of your monthly income, a private mortgage insurance company would want to see your monthly mortgage payment not to exceed 25% of your monthly income. Similarly, a lender might be willing to excuse a couple of late payments on your credit history but a PMI might not. In other words, you need a good credit history and good income in order to qualify for PMI.

Can You Remove the PMI Coverage?

Now let's explore one other area. What happens when you have paid down your mortgage sufficiently so that your outstanding balance on the loan is only 75% or 80% of the mortgage you had originally incurred. Say, for example, you had taken out a mortgage for 95% of the value of the property and had 20% PMI coverage. After several years your mortgage is now paid down to 75% of the original value. Can you get rid of the PMI coverage?

In most cases, you can, since the PMI covered only the top 20% of the loan. Now that you have paid down your loan by 20%, there's no reason for you to pay that extra 1/4 point to carry the PMI. By getting rid of the PMI at this point you'll be able to save a nifty sum of money every month.

But what happens if your mortgage has not been paid down to 75% of the original value but, due to appreciation in the property value, the outstanding loan balance is 75% or less than the fair market value of the property?

Can you still get rid of the PMI in that case? Most probably not. For reasons that are hard to understand, most lenders and mortgage institutions do not look at the market value of the property to decide whether a private mortgage is required or not. Even though the property value may have risen considerably over the years they will not waive the PMI coverage just on those grounds. They would still require you to reduce your outstanding balance to 75 or 70% of the original amount borrowed before dropping the PMI requirement.

Conclusion

In conclusion, PMI may be helpful to many borrowers. In fact, it may be the only way some people can afford to buy a home. When an individual has not saved enough money to put more than 5% down on a home he has no recourse but to look for a PMI in order to persuade a lender to allow him to borrow 95% of the value of the property. For many real estate investors too, PMI is an easy way to be able to obtain loans on non-owner occupied properties.

Refinancing 15

In the old days, it used to be that mortgage rates never fluctuated more than a fraction of a point even as the economic conditions changed. Mortgages were written for thirty years and homeowners hung on to their mortgages till they were fully paid off or till they sold their homes. Those days are now a memory of the past.

These days mortgage interest rates are quoted on a daily basis. Most major newspapers report current mortgage rates on a weekly basis. Banks and other mortgage institutions immediately react to interest rate developments in other sectors of the economy by adjusting their mortgage interest rates. Even after a lender has made a commitment to lend money to a borrower at a certain interest rate, the commitment is good for only a limited period of time, typically 30 days. After this period, the lender reserves the right to adjust the offered rate. The idea behind this interest rate sensitivity is the desire of every lender to match closely its cost of funds with the return it expects to earn by lending the money to a mortgagor.

Whether To Refinance or Not

The depth and frequency of interest rate swings in recent years has created a dilemma for many a homeowner. You may have bought your home at a time when interest rate was 17% and presently it is hovering around 9%. Should you refinance your mortgage to lower your monthly payments?

Of course, the decision in this particular case is easy. But how do you know exactly when it makes economic sense to refinance a mortgage?

There are many situations that may prompt you to look at refinancing alternative. Your original mortgage is an adjustable rate mortgage (ARM), and now you wish to convert it to a fixed rate mortgage just so that you do not get whipsawed when the interest rates do go back up. On the other hand, you want to convert your fixed rate mortgage to an ARM so that you can take advantage of continually decreasing interest rates.

A homeowner facing any of these situations has to make the critical decision: Whether to refinance the current mortgage or not.

Factors Affecting Refinancing

Let's examine various factors that affect refinancing decision.

1. Interest rate on your current mortgage

This often is the threshold question. If the interest rate on your mortgage is at least 2 points higher than a currently-available mortgage, you might want to consider refinancing. In some cases, you'll need at least a 3-point differential before it will make economic sense to refinance. We'll look at the costs involved in refinancing a mortgage later in this chapter, but suffice it is to say that they are substantial. The savings you expect to obtain through lower monthly payments must offset these costs, - and that depends on the length of time you intend to occupy your home.

2. Length of time you intend to hold the property

Having refinanced the property, you'll need to hold it sufficiently long to recoup the costs of refinancing. If you intend to hold it for a long period, a two point interest differential may be enough to justify refinancing. If the holding period is going to be shorter, you may have to look for a three point or even greater differential before deciding to refinance.

Illustration: Say you're presently holding a $125,000 mortgage which was originally financed at 13.5% fixed rate interest. Your monthly payments on this 30-year mortgage are $1,431.77. Presently you are in a position to obtain a like-amount mortgage at 9% interest rate. Your new monthly payments will be $1,005.78 giving you a monthly saving of $425.99. In one year you'll save $5,111.88. The refinancing will roughly cost you $3,000 in loan origination fees, escrow charges and other settlement costs. Under these circumstances, you'll recoup your refinancing costs in approximately seven months. This undoubtedly is an attractive option for the homeowner.

3. ARM or fixed rate mortgage

Next to a precipitous drop in interest rates, this is another reason that induces many homeowners to refinance their mortgages. Adjustable rate mortgages have become very popular in recent years. They generally have a lower initial interest rate (the so-called "teaser rate") and, therefore, are easier to qualify for. However, they carry with them the uncertainty of potential future hikes in interest rates. With an ARM, a homeowner may someday face the possibility of monthly mortgage payments that are beyond his means. Rather than live with this uncertainty, he may like to refinance his mortgage and convert it to a fixed rate mortgage.

Here, of course, the consideration is not lower monthly payment. It is the security of knowing that your mortgage payments are not going to change in the future by events beyond your control.

On the other hand, a homeowner who had obtained a fixed rate mortgage at a high interest rate may be inclined to convert it to an adjustable rate mortgage to benefit from lower monthly payments. If the interest rates are in general decline, such a course of action would be advisable. The trade-off, of course, is the loss of security of fixed rate mortgage against lower monthly outlay.

4. Your current financial position

Refinancing is very much like obtaining a new loan. The lender, even if he happens to be the same one holding the current mortgage, would want to see your credit history, length of employment, income and outstanding debts. In short, you have to qualify for the refinanced loan just as you had qualified for the original loan. If you have just started a new job or are in the process of going into business independently, it may be harder to qualify for the loan. You may have no option but to continue with the current loan.

5. Tapping your equity in the house

There's yet another factor that prompts many homeowners to refinance their property. Over the years, with the soaring real estate market in general, many homeowners have discovered that they are sitting on a large sum of money in the form of a built-up equity in their homes. Their original loan, obtained years ago at a very low interest rate, has probably been paid down to a point where monthly mortgage payments are not a burden. Their main objective in refinancing is to tap the equity that is sitting idle in the home. The funds thus released can be used for other purposes, such as alternative investments, travel, vacation home, etc.

Refinancing is not without its tax benefits. Any amount that is left over after paying off existing obligations will be a tax-free boot to the owner. The cash taken out as proceeds of the loan is not taxed to the owner as against a sale or other disposition of the property would. To the extent that the new debt exceeds the original financing, refinancing reduces the owner's equity in the property.

Cost of Refinancing

Refinancing is costly. The actual procedure is not much different than that involved in obtaining a new loan. You go through essentially the same steps that you went through when you bought your home.

As a rule of thumb, refinancing will cost you anywhere from two and one-half to three points and, in some cases, higher on the borrowed amount. The following is a brief summary of various costs involved.

Points or Loan Origination Fee   This is a fee imposed by the lender and increases lender's interest yield. Generally, the points charged will vary from one to five points depending upon various factors, such as your credit rating, loan-to-value ratio, whether it is an owner-occupied house or not, etc. This is the single largest expense involved in refinancing.

Title Insurance   Lender will require you to obtain a new title insurance policy at your expense. Depending upon the size of the loan, this may cost you anywhere from $200 to $500, or more.

Escrow Refinancing involves escrow just as the home purchase did originally. Expect to pay $200 to $400 in the form of escrow fee.

Document Preparation Fee Escrow company will charge you to prepare certain documents such as deed of trust, note etc. Cost: $25-$50.

Document Recording Fee   The documents that need to be recorded with the city or county recorder's office. Cost: $10-$20.

Credit Report   Lender will run a credit check which may cost you approximately $35.

Appraisal Fee   Most lenders will charge you to appraise the property. They'll employ one of their own appraisers and the cost of appraisal may run about $250 to $500. The lender may limit the amount of the loan to no more than 70% to 80% of the appraised value. Some conservative lenders may even restrict themselves to a lower amount.

Tax Service Fee   This usually runs about $25 and is paid to a company to notify the lender in the event you default on your property taxes.

Termite Inspection Fee   Most lenders will require you to produce a clear termite report from an authorized termite inspection company. This may cost you in the range of $100. If the termite report uncovers any areas that need to be worked upon, the corrective action will cost you extra.

Impound Account   A few lenders may require an impound account which means that you pay taxes and insurance on a monthly basis along with the principal and interest. This advance payment of taxes and insurance may create an additional burden for you.

In many cases, you'll not have to pay out of your pocket the above expenses of refinancing. The lender will allow you to amortize these expenses over the term of the loan; you'll actually be borrowing these expenses which in turn reduces the proceeds of the loan.

Illustration: Based on the appraisal of the house and your credit, the lender has agreed to lend you $80,000. The cost of refinancing has been estimated at $2,800. The lender will deduct these costs from the loan proceeds, reducing them to $77,200. Your new mortgage payments will be based on $80,000.

Actual Example

Shown in the table below are the actual costs of refinancing an $80,000 loan. It cost $3,357.94 to refinance this sum. Typically, part of the proceeds of refinancing would go to pay off the existing obligations, and excess, if any, would be handed over to the borrower.

Incidentally, refinancing the mortgage in this particular case was done to pay off the balloon payment that had become due on a note secured by the second deed of trust. The property had appreciated over the years and the owner wanted to tap the sizeable equity that had built up. The new mortgage payments were considerably higher, but the refinancing made available a large sum of money for other investments.

Illustration of Refinancing Costs
Refinanced Amount: $80,000.00

Loan Origination Fee	$1,700.00
Tax Service Contract	20.00
Prepaid Interest	513.94
Prepaid Hazard Insurance	264.00
Escrow Fee	235.00
Loan Demand Fee	50.00
Title Insurance	480.00
Reconveyance Fee	40.00
Sub-Escrow Fee	35.00
Recording Fee	15.00
Trustee Fee	5.00
Total Refinancing Cost	**$3,357.94**

Should you Refinance?

This chapter has given you all the considerations involved in making the decision to refinance or not. Shop around for the best rates and terms from a lender. Obtain from the lender an approximation of the costs involved in refinancing. A lender is required by law to give you a good-faith estimate of the settlement charges. Compute your savings from possible lower payments. Review your own plans as to how long you intend to hold the property. Using the examples and procedures shown here, prepare a breakeven analysis to help you make the final decision.

Refinancing to Improve Salability of Property

Refinancing can be used to make a property more attractive to a prospective buyer. Very often a seller would obtain the highest possible mortgage on a property before putting it on the market. The new mortgage is obtained with an eye toward making it assumable by the buyer of the property. This would avoid the risk that financing may not be available at the time the sale is consummated or that the prospective buyer may not qualify for a new loan on his own. Refinancing may also make the sale go through faster since the buyer is assuming an existing loan or taking it over "subject to," rather than obtaining a new loan.

If the refinancing could be obtained at an interest rate lower than what is being paid on the existing mortgage the prospective buyer would benefit additionally: he would be buying a highly leveraged property at a lower interest rate. Even in cases where refinancing is possible only at a higher interest rate, it may still be beneficial to the buyer. We'll illustrate this in the following example.

Illustration: Let us say that a owner has put up for sale a $1 million apartment house that has a net operating income of $100,000. For him, the return on total investment in the property is 10%. Let's also assume that the property has a first mortgage of $500,000 at 8% interest, which requires annual payments of $45,000. The mortgage has been paid down to $300,000.

There are three alternatives available to the owner.

1. He can sell the property for all cash. This means that a prospective buyer would be required to come up with $1 million dollars in cash. This would be a very difficult proposition and may not be feasible in many cases.

2. The seller may decide to sell the property subject to the existing mortgage. The buyer would assume the existing mortgage of $300,000 and would put up $700,000 as down payment. This amount, though not beyond the means of some buyers, would definitely limit the range of the possible market. For the buyer, the return on his investment of $700,000 would be 7.85% which is arrived at by taking the net operating income, subtracting from it the debt service of $45,000 and dividing the result by the buyer's cash investment in the property of $700,000. Even if you assume that the rents can be raised in the near future so that the cash flow jumps to $75,000 from $55,000, the cash flow return for the buyer would still be a little less than 11% ($75,000 on an investment of $700,000.)

3. As a third alternative, the seller can obtain a new first mortgage before putting the property up for sale in the amount of $700,000 at 10% interest requiring annual mortgage payments of $84,000. In this case the buyer would be required to come up with only $300,000 in cash.

Right off, you're going to attract many more buyers under these terms. The cash flow under the new mortgage would be $16,000 ($100,000 of net operating income minus $84,000 in mortgage payments.) For the buyer, this amounts to a return of 5.33%, on cash flow basis. If we assume that the rents can be increased by $20,000 so that the cash flow would raise to $36,000, the cash flow return would jump to 12%, which is higher than under any of the above two alternatives.

Refinancing makes the property more saleable to an investor by:

a) reducing the amount of cash required;

b) raising the cash flow yield to the new investor;

c) increasing the tax shelter since a much higher mortgage is now available as tax deductible interest.

Impact of Tax Reform on You as a Homeowner

Deductibility of mortgage interest and real property taxes has been the driving force behind sustained real estate activity in America for the past several decades. The 1986 Tax Reform Act phased out many categories of itemized deductions for personal interest, but left intact the deductibility of interest on debt secured by a taxpayer's principal residence or a second residence. Thus the lure and impetus to invest in real estate is still present for most first-time home buyers.

Refinancing Under 1986 Tax Reform Act

Under the 1986 Tax Reform, but prior to certain modifications enacted under the Revenue and Pension Protection Act of 1987, interest on debt secured by a person's principal or a second residence was deductible only to the extent that it did not exceed his cost basis (including the cost of home improvement.) If the proceeds of refinancing were used for educational or medical expenses, the interest on this borrowed amount was also tax deductible.

Modifications Under 1987 Tax Act

The 1987 Act redefines qualified residence interest to include two categories of interest with respect to a principal or second residence: interest on acquisition indebtedness and interest on home equity indebtedness.

Acquisition Indebtedness. The maximum amount of mortgage interest you can deduct on your principal and a second residence is limited to the interest on $1 million indebtedness.   In other words, if the debt to acquire, construct or substantially improve a principal and second residence exceeds $1,000,000, then only the interest on a total principal amount of $1,000,000 is deductible as interest on acquisition indebtedness.

Illustration: Say you're buying a home in 1988 as your principal residence. The first mortgage held by a bank amounts to $600,000 at 9%. The seller has provided secondary financing in the amount of $300,000 at 12% interest. In 1989 you purchase a second residence and incur indebtedness of $350,000 at 11% interest. Under the new rules, your interest deductions will be limited to the first $1,000,000 indebtedness. Although the interest paid on the first and second mortgages on your primary residence is fully deductible since it is below the $1,000,000 limit, you'll be able to deduct interest only on the $100,000 debt at 11% that you incurred in acquiring your second residence.

Home Equity Indebtedness. The new rules also allow you to deduct interest on any home equity loan you may obtain to the extent that this amount does not exceed $100,000. There's one more restriction: The combined total of acquisition indebtedness and home equity indebtedness cannot exceed the fair market value of the residence. Further, the total amount of home equity indebtedness and acquisition indebtedness on a principal and second residence cannot exceed $1,100,000. There is, however, no restriction on how you use the proceeds of the home equity loan.

Illustration: Presently you own your home that has a fair market value of $600,000. You purchased the property at a cost of $300,000 and, over the years, you've spent $50,000 to substantially improve the property. Your cost basis, therefore, is $350,000. You take out an home equity loan in the sum of $120,000 at 12%. Under the new rules, you'll be allowed to deduct interest on this home equity loan to the extent of $100,000.

Illustration: You bought a home for $500,000 and paid the mortgage down to $200,000. Under the Tax Reform Act of 1986, you could refinance the mortgage for up to $500,000 and get a full interest deduction. But under the 1987 Act, you can claim an interest deduction on a refinancing for only up to $300,000 ($200,000 on the existing mortgage plus $100,000 of new debt.)

Impact: These new limits generally cut back on the opportunity to use home loans to finance consumer purchases and other expenses. In the future, home buyers who wish to use home loans to maximize their deductible borrowing should take out the largest mortgages possible (up to the $1 million aggregate) over the longest term.

Hidden benefit: There's good news in the new borrowing limits, too. Subject to the $1 million cap, you can deduct interest on up to $100,000 of increased financing against your home regardless of the home's original cost. Thus, if the cost plus improvements of your home were $300,000 and you have paid the mortgage down to $250,000, you can borrow another $100,000 to make your total debt $350,000. Under the pre-1987 Tax Act rules you could borrow only another $50,000 so that debt equaled the home's cost (including improvements) of $300,000 unless amounts in excess of $300,000 were for educational or medical expenses.

Real Estate and Taxes

16

Real estate in America has always been driven by its tax advantages, as opposed to stock, bonds or other kinds of investments. Historically, our public policy has promoted home ownership. Even after the 1986 Tax Reform Act that did away with a wide range of tax loopholes, real estate investments continue to retain their appeal from tax standpoint. By all standards, tax and economic benefits of owning real estate far outweigh similar benefits from other investments. In this chapter, we'll examine the tax consequences of investing in real estate, whether it be your home or other income-producing property.

Investment in Real Estate

The case for investing in income-producing real estate can be based on three separate propositions.

One: A good real estate investment will not only produce above average annual cash flow but also long-term appreciation in its market value.

Two: Under the current tax law, real estate investments alone offer the most favorable tax treatment for an average investor. The tax benefits that have been retained range from deductibility of mortgage interest for the principal and second home to the ability to offset rental real estate losses up to $25,000 against a taxpayer's other income under certain circumstances.

Three: The advantage of leverage. Real estate can be bought with only the minimal down payment while borrowing a very large amount against it. This financial leverage acts to magnify several times the basic economic and tax benefits to a real estate investor.

New Tax Law

In a large measure, the Tax Reform Act of 1986 put a crimp on the tax benefits of owning real estate. For one, the ability to use losses from real estate investments to shelter your other income has been severely curtailed by the new law. Further, the depreciation schedules have been tightened so that the period over which buildings may be depreciated has been substantially stretched out. The long term capital gains rate has been made equal to the regular tax rate so that the advantage of owning real estate and selling it at a later date to minimize your gains has been eliminated. And finally, the right to report gain from the sale of property under the installment method is also significantly reduced.

But the picture isn't entirely bleak. A number of significant tax benefits that existed under the prior law have been continued under the new law. Let's briefly look at a few of these tax consequences, some beneficial and some detrimental to a homeowner or real estate investor.

Deduction of Home Mortgage Interest

While eliminating the deduction for most personal interest expenses, Congress decided to retain the deduction for interest on debt secured by a taxpayer's principal and a second residence. The ability to deduct interest on a home mortgage loan is an important consideration for many families contemplating the purchase of their home.

Under pre-1987 Tax Act law, but subsequent to the 1986 Tax Reform, interest on debts secured by a taxpayer's principal residence or a second residence was generally deductible to the extent that the debt does not exceed the amount of the taxpayer's basis in the residence (including the cost of home improvements.) The interest on certain mortgage debts incurred to meet educational or medical expenses was also included in the qualified residence interest.

The 1987 Act redefines qualified residence interest to include two categories of interest with respect to a principal or second residence - interest on acquisition indebtedness and interest on home equity indebtedness. The maximum amount of acquisition indebtedness allowed under the law is $1 million, and home equity indebtedness cannot exceed $100,000. Under a grandfather provision, pre-October 14, 1987 mortgage debt regardless of amount is treated as acquisition indebtedness.

Acquisition Indebtedness

Acquisition indebtedness is debt that is incurred in acquiring, constructing, or substantially improving the principal or a second residence of the taxpayer and which is secured by the residence. If a taxpayer refinances his acquisition indebtedness, the new debt is acquisition indebtedness, but only to the extent that it does not exceed the balance of the old debt. In other words, a taxpayer who refinances his home cannot take out additional cash from the transaction and have it count as acquisition indebtedness.

Also, as you pay down your mortgage your acquisition indebtedness is reduced and it cannot be increased by refinancing. For example, say you have a $100,000 acquisition indebtedness, which over a period of time is reduced by payments of principal to $80,000. Acquisition indebtedness cannot thereafter be increased above $80,000 unless the purpose of refinancing was to substantially improve the residence.

As we said above, the amount of mortgage interest that can be deducted is limited to acquisition indebtedness of $1 million. In other words, if you acquire, construct, or substantially improve a principal or second residence, and your cost exceeds $1 million, then only the interest on a total principal amount of $1 million is deductible as interest on acquisition indebtedness.

Illustration: Say a taxpayer purchases a principal residence in 1988 and obtains a mortgage from a bank for $600,000 at 9% interest; the seller took back a $300,000 purchase money mortgage with interest at 10%. In 1989 the taxpayer purchases a second residence and incurs a mortgage debt of $350,000 at 12% interest.

Under the new rules, the aggregate debt on the two residences to the extent that it doesn't exceed $1 million will qualify as acquisition indebtedness. Thus, with the mortgage on the first residence being $900,000, only $100,000 of the debt on the second residence will qualify as acquisition indebtedness. The additional $250,000 indebtedness will not qualify for mortgage interest deduction.

Home Equity Indebtedness

Interest on home equity indebtedness is also deductible interest. Home equity indebtedness is debt secured by a taxpayer's principal or second residence to the extent the aggregate amount of such indebtedness does not exceed the fair market value of the residence reduced by the amount of acquisition indebtedness with respect to the residence. In other words, the combined total of acquisition indebtedness and home equity indebtedness cannot exceed the fair market value of the residence.

The 1987 law does not impose any restriction on how you use the proceeds of the home equity indebtedness. The law does, however, say that the amount of debt that is treated as home equity indebtedness cannot exceed $100,000. To put it another way, the total amount of home equity indebtedness on a principal and second residence when combined with the acquisition indebtedness on these residences cannot exceed $1.1 million.

Passive Losses

Under the new law all business and investment activities are put into one of three categories:

One: Active trade or business activity

Two: Portfolio activity

Three: Passive activity

For tax years beginning after 1986, passive losses and credits may only be used to offset passive income. They cannot offset income from active sources, such as a business or profession actively carried on by the taxpayer or his salary. Nor can they be used to offset portfolio income, such as interest, dividends, stock gains, etc.

A tax loss created by an active trade or business may be used to offset other income, just as you were able to do under the previous law. Similarly, losses from portfolio activities such as stocks and option trading may offset gains from such activities plus up to $3,000 annually of other income.

As a result of these limitations on deductibility of passive losses against active income, real estate investments have been hit the hardest. For instance, a real estate investment property such as an office building or an apartment house may very often generate a tax loss for the year. This loss under the previous law could be used to offset any taxable income of the taxpayer such as salary, dividends, net capital gains and so forth. Under the new rules you'll not be able to do this.

Illustration: For example, you own an office building on which your gross rental income is $100,000 and your operating expenses amount to $110,000. You, therefore, realize an economic loss for the year of $10,000. Unless you qualify for the special $25,000 exception (explained below), this $10,000 loss is a passive loss and can be used to offset only other passive income. It can no longer be used to reduce your salary or portfolio incomes.

Under the new rules all real estate rental activities regardless of the individual taxpayer's participation are considered passive activities. It does, however, provide one important exception in its treatment of passive losses to offset other active income.

Active Participation Exception

A taxpayer, who owns at least a 10% interest in the property and satisfies an "active participation" requirement, can use up to $25,000 of real estate losses to offset other income, such as salary or dividends. The taxpayer, however, must actively participate in the real estate rental activity. The $25,000 deduction is reduced by 50% of the taxpayer's adjusted gross income in excess of $100,000. In other words, the $25,000 deduction is phased out between $100,000 and $150,000 of income. Thus, when a taxpayer has $150,000 of aggregate gross income, he loses this right to deduct any real estate losses.

Active Participation. What is active participation?

The active participation standard imposed by the IRS is intended to be less stringent than the material participation requirement. The active participation requirement can be satisfied without regular, continuous and substantial involvement in operations so long as the taxpayer participates in a significant way by, for example, making management decisions or arranging for others to provide service.

Management decisions that are relevant in determining whether a taxpayer actively participates include approving new tenants, deciding on rental terms, approving capital or repair expenditures and other similar decisions.

For example, a taxpayer who owns and rents out an apartment that formerly was his primary residence, or one that he uses as a part time vacation home, may be considered as actively participating even if he hires a rental agent and others provide services such as repairs as long as he participates by making vital management decisions. On the other hand, a taxpayer who makes no significant decisions isn't likely to qualify. For example, if you buy an interest in a deal promoted as a tax shelter, under which all significant management decisions are left to a management company, you are not likely to qualify as an active participant.

General Phase-in Rule

The passive loss rule, as described above, is being phased-in over 5 years. During the phase-in period, instead of 100% of the excess passive losses being disallowed, the following percentage of losses will be disallowed:

1987	35%
1988	60%
1989	80%
1990	90%

In 1991 and thereafter, 100% of passive losses will be disallowed.

Illustration: Say, in 1987, you were a limited partner in two real estate partnerships. In Partnership A you had a tax loss of $10,000 after subtracting gross rental income from operating expenses, mortgage interest and depreciation deductions. In Partnership B you had a taxable income of $5,000.

Under the new rules, you'll be able to offset $5,000 of your loss in Partnership A against the $5,000 gain in Partnership B. Of the remaining $5,000 loss, in 1987, you'll be able to offset only 65%, that is, $3,250 to reduce other outside income. The remaining $1,750 is added to your tax basis for your interest in Partnership A.

If, in 1988, you again have a net passive loss of $5,000 from Partnership A, only 40% of that loss, that is, $2,000, could be used to offset outside income. The remaining loss of $3,000 is added to your tax basis for your interest in Partnership A.

In 1991 and thereafter, none of the passive losses could be used to offset outside income. Instead, the losses would have to be carried forward.

For example, if, in 1991, you had a passive loss on your Partnership A of $2,000 and a net passive loss of $3,000 against Partnership B, a total of $5,000 in passive losses would be carried forward. When the partnership is terminated the excess loss attributable to the partnership could be used to offset outside income such as salary. In other words, the disallowed losses are allowed in full against all categories of the taxpayer's income in the year in which he disposes of his entire interest in the activity in a fully taxable transaction.

Unused passive credits, unlike passive losses, can only be offset against tax arising from future passive income from other passive activities owned by the taxpayer.

Illustration: As we've observed above, when you dispose of your interest in any passive activity any disposition gain or loss plus carry forward losses with respect to that activity are allowed in full. However, to the extent that the loss on the disposition is deemed to arise from the sale or exchange of a capital asset, it can be used only to offset other capital gains plus $3,000 from ordinary income. In other words, a capital loss does not become free of the capital loss limitation merely because it also is a passive loss.

For example, in 1991 you have a capital loss of $10,000 when you dispose of a passive activity. And, you also have a $5,000 carry forward losses arising from the same activity. Under the rules, the $5,000 of carry forward ordinary losses are allowed in full against other income but the capital loss from $10,000 can be used only to offset other capital gains for the year plus $3,000 of ordinary income. Any unused capital loss is carried forward and may be used to offset capital gain plus $3,000 of ordinary income in future years.

Who Is Subject to Passive Tax Limits?

The rule limiting the allowability of passive activity losses and credits applies to individuals, estates, trusts, closely held C corporations and personal service corporations. It does not apply to partnerships or S corporations, but applies to losses passed through to partners or shareholders.

A closely held C corporation is any C corporation more than 50% in value of whose stock is owned by 5 or fewer individuals. There is a special rule that applies to C corporations. A closely held C corporation that isn't a personal service corporation may offset passive losses against "net active income," but not against portfolio income. A personal service corporation cannot offset passive losses against either active income or portfolio income.

Illustration: A closely held corporation has $400,000 of passive losses from a real estate rental activity, $500,000 of active business income, and $100,000 of portfolio income. The passive losses of $400,000 can be used to reduce the active business income to $100,000, but it cannot be used to offset any portfolio income. If, on the other hand, the corporation had $500,000 in passive losses from the rental activity, $400,000 in active business income and $100,000 in portfolio income, the passive loss can only offset the business income of $400,000, but not the portfolio income. As a result, the corporation would be left with a nondeductible $100,000 in passive losses and $100,000 in portfolio income.

Tax Reform Act of 1986 Passive Loss Restrictions

Can passive losses be used against

	Active Business	Portfolio
1. Individual	No	No
2. Personal service corporation	No	No
3. Closely held C corporation	Yes	No
4. C corporation (other than 2 or 3)	Yes	Yes

Depreciation

Until the Tax Reform Act of 1986, the approved system for depreciating real property was the accelerated cost recovery system (ACRS) which applied to property placed in service after December 31, 1980. Under those rules all depreciable real estate except low income housing placed in service prior to January 1, 1987 was depreciated over 19 years.

Under the Tax Reform Act of 1986, new rules apply to the computation of depreciation for properties placed in service after December 31, 1986.

All residential real property is now depreciated in a straight-line manner over 27 1/2 years. For non- residential real property the method of depreciation is straight-line over 31 1/2 years. For both residential and non-residential property, the depreciation for the initial and final year of ownership is based on the number of months the property is in service during the taxable year and for this purpose a mid-month convention applies. That is, the property is treated as having been placed in service or disposed of in the middle of the month.

Vacation Homes

Many people own vacation homes that are used partly for personal use and partly for rental to others. Under the Tax Reform Act of 1986, new rules apply to the treatment of income and expenses attributed to vacation homes. In order to understand these rules, vacation homes can be divided into three categories:

1. **Limited rental use**

2. **Limited personal use**

3. **Substantial rental and personal use**

Limited Rental Use

If the vacation home is rented for less than 15 days during the taxable year, no deductions attributable to the rental are allowable and no income derived from the rental need be included in gross income. The IRS recognizes neither deductions nor income in these situations because the relative amounts are too small. As a result, the vacation home which is used for rental less than 15 days in a year is treated more as a personal residence.

If the vacation home is the taxpayer's first or second residence, under the rules, mortgage interest can be taken as an itemized deduction. However, if it is a third residence, interest is treated as if it is consumer interest; that is, the interest is non-deductible after 1990 and deductible in part until then in accordance with the phase-in rules.

Limited Personal Use

If the vacation home is rented for 15 or more days during the taxable year and personal use by the owner is limited to not more than 14 days, or, if greater, not more than 10% of the rental days, the house is classified as business property and not a residence of the owner. All expenses including depreciation associated with the vacation home then must be allocated between rental use and personal use. In allocating expense and depreciation, except mortgage interest, you can use the ratio, days rented to the total days of rental and personal use.

Illustration: Let us say that you own a vacation home which you use for 14 days for your personal use and rent it out to others for 100 days. In this case, the ratio applicable to rental use is 88%, that is, 100 days divided by 114 days; the ratio for personal use is 12%, that is, 14 days divided by 114 days. With regards to mortgage interest and real estate taxes you should be able to use the ratio arrived at by dividing the rental days by 365 days.

The amount of expenses plus depreciation allocated to rental use is deductible in accordance with the passive loss rules of the Tax Reform Act of 1986 as we described earlier. Briefly, if the gross rental receipt is greater than allocable expenses and depreciation, the excess is taxable income. If the gross rental is less than the allocable expenses and depreciation, the loss is a passive loss deductible only against passive income.

Again, the special phase-in rules applicable to the years between 1987 and 1990 will be applicable to offset outside income against this passive income. Also, a taxpayer who qualifies for the special $25,000 exception to the passive loss limitation would be able to offset this loss against his other outside income. The amount of expense less depreciation allocated to personal use is not deductible except for real estate taxes. The mortgage interest is not deductible because the limited personal use prevents the vacation home from being treated as a qualified second residence. Thus, mortgage interest allocated to the personal use of the house is considered non-deductible consumer interest.

Substantial Rental and Personal Use

There may be cases where an owner may use his vacation home more than allowed under the limited personal use situation and may also rent the property which may be greater than allowed under the limited rental use. In other words, the vacation home is now both a qualified second residence for the purpose of deducting mortgage interest and also a business property for which expenses and depreciation may be deducted to the extent of rental income.

In this situation, the vacation home owner must first allocate all expenses plus depreciation between business and personal use in accordance with the rules we have just described above. Then, the expenses and depreciation allocated to the business use are deductible up to the amount of rental income. The mortgage interest attributed to the personal use is deductible if the house is a qualified personal residence. The real estate taxes allocated to the personal use are deductible.

Conclusion: As a result of the restrictive passive loss rules of the Tax Reform Act of 1986, if you own a vacation home, you might be better off making substantial personal use of the home rather than using it solely for rental.

Intra-Family Transactions

It is not unusual for children to borrow money from their parents to buy their home. It also is not uncommon for parents to live in a home owned by the children and pay rent to them. However, such intra-family transactions should be handled very carefully in order to avoid an attack by the IRS which may disallow deductions to the owner.

Taxpayer Victory

A recent case involving sale-and-leaseback arrangement within the family was decided in favor of the taxpayer. But a slight change of facts could have altered the outcome.

In 1979, a Virginia dentist borrowed money from his parents to buy a townhouse as an investment. He gave his parents a promissory note, bearing a 12% interest, payable twice a year, with all principal due after five years. He made the scheduled interest payments and his parents declared the interest as income on there tax return. Later in the same year, the dentist's parents retired and moved to Virginia. He rented the townhouse to them for $550 a month which was the fair market rental in the area. The doctor kept meticulous records of the rental agreement and the rents paid by his parents. The lease agreement provided for periodic increases in rent to keep up with the market value. In spite of this, the IRS tried to tie the two deals together, his borrowing of money from his parents to buy the townhouse and later, renting the same property to his parents, and labeled them as a sham transaction.

The Tax Court disagreed after looking at the evidence produced by the son that the property was managed as a business and was not a tax avoidance device. The loan procured from the parents was a bonafide loan and the business was conducted as an arms-length transaction. The Court upheld the deductions taken by the dentist on the investment property even though the property was rented within the family.

How to Tap the Equity in Your Home

Here's the flip side of the above deal. Often parents own a property which has appreciated considerably over the years; however, they do not have any regular income to meet their monthly expenses.

Let us say that parents own a home which was bought several years ago at a cost of $45,000; the mortgage has been paid off and $45,000 is the adjusted cost basis for them. The parents are living on a small pension and social security income. However, this income is not sufficient to meet their regular living expenses. The house is appraised at a fair market value of $170,000. In short, the parents are sitting on a lot of equity which they cannot convert to cash. They do not want to sell the house and look for another place to rent for the remaining years of their lives. So, what is the solution?

In situations such as this, a deal can be structured enabling the parents to continue to live in the house where they have lived for several years, and still convert the large amount of equity accumulated in the house into a stream of regular cash flow.

The adult child of the parents can buy the house from his parents and give them a lifetime lease. The sale price would be the fair market value of the house which would provide the parents with $125,000 capital gain. This gain would be tax free to them because of the once-in-a-lifetime exclusion on the sale of their principal residence. As far as the son is concerned, he can start taking depreciation on the property on his cost basis and take deductions for mortgage interest, taxes, repairs, and maintenance and any other associated expenses. Under the new tax law, he can write off up to $25,000 of his losses against the adjusted gross income of as much as $100,000. By structuring the deal in this manner, both parties can come out ahead; the house stays in the family, the parents get to continue to live in the house, and the son has obtained a viable tax shelter.

Record Keeping for IRS

How long should you maintain your records about your home purchase, cost of improvements, refinancing, etc.?

As a rule, you need to maintain your records about your home not only for annual tax purposes, but also for determining your gain or loss at the time you sell your property several years in the future. The IRS regulations require you to maintain records of any capital improvements you may have made in your home, any home equity loans you may have taken out, or other financing you may have obtained on the home. If you own several properties, including rental properties, you would need to maintain a file containing all these records for each one of your properties.

Your files should include the original price of the home and closing or settlement costs, by way of interest points paid at the time of closing, title insurance, legal fees, escrow fees, recording fees, etc. If you've made any improvements in your home, such as adding a new floor, putting in a patio or swimming pool, or making additions to your home, you must maintain a record of these improvements in your file. The capital improvements made to your home would be depreciated over the life of the home, and at the time of the sale would have to be taken into account in order to arrive at your capital gain or loss as the case may be.

If you make routine repairs to your home, such as painting, wall papering, plumbing, etc, they are not considered capital improvements. These are on-going maintenance and repair expenses which are expensed out in the year you incur them. They will not affect any gains or losses incurred on the home at the time of sale. To make your job easy, you may want to prepare a schedule showing the original cost of the home, and improvements made by date, the nature of improvement, the cost of improvement, and other pertinent information.

Tax Advantages When You Sell Your Home

17

Your home is more than just a place for you to live. It is also the most important investment you'll make during your lifetime. Barring a few exceptional times, real estate values have always risen bringing windfall gains to the homeowner. What most homeowners know, and have come to accept, is that Uncle Sam is an important partner in this investment. By a shrewd use of the tax law, you'll be able to keep the gains to yourself without having to share them with Uncle Sam.

Two Ways to Save on Taxes

Current tax law permits to avoid tax on any gain realized upon sale of their home in two major ways:

1. When you sell your present home and acquire a replacement residence which costs as much or more than the sale price of the old residence, you can defer taxes on the gains realized from the sale.

2. The law allows an individual, 55 or older, to exclude up to $125,000 in gain from the sale of his principal residence.

Under the 1986 Tax Reform Act, any gain not absorbed by the deferral or one-time exemption is taxable as ordinary income at 28% rate.

How to Defer Taxes on the Sale of Your Residence

The law gives any homeowner, regardless of age, a special tax break when he sells his home at a profit and replaces it by buying or constructing another residence within a specified period. Below are some of the particulars and requirements of the law.

Principal Residence

The deferral of tax on gain applies only to the taxpayer's principal residence. It does not apply to summer home, vacation home or some other dwelling that is not used as your principal residence. The principal residence can be a boat, mobile home, house trailer, an apartment or condominium.

Occupancy

There is no requirement that you must have occupied the principal residence for a certain minimum period. It is also not necessary that you must be living in the principal residence at the time of sale. You could rent the residence for a temporary period while in the process of selling it and not lose the tax advantage of deferral of gains.

The law requires that you physically occupy the new home. Merely moving your furniture or other personal belongings into that new home without actually occupying it will not work.

Time Limits to Replace

To defer tax on profit, the residence which is sold must be replaced within the period specified by law.

If you replace by purchasing another home (whether brand new or used), you must buy and use the replacement residence by occupying it within the period beginning two years before sale of the old residence and ending two years after sale of the old residence.

If you replace by building a new home, you have until two years after sale of the old home to finish and occupy the home.

If a new residence is purchased before an individual sells his old residence, temporarily renting out the new residence will not necessarily prevent it from being considered as property used as his principal residence.

Observation: The residences do not have to be in the same country. Thus, purchase of a replacement home abroad qualifies.

Computing the Gain to be Deferred

The homeowner is taxed on his profit in the year of sale only to the extent that the adjusted sales price of the old residence exceeds the cost of the replacement residence.

The adjusted sales price of the old home is the gross selling price reduced by (1) expenses of sale (lawyer's fees, commissions, etc.) and (2) any "fixing-up" expenses (painting, papering, etc.) incurred for work done within the 90-day period before the sales contract is entered into and paid within 30 days after the sale date.

The cost of the replacement residence that you purchase includes sales commissions and other purchasing expenses, plus any additions or improvements that are added to the replacement residence between one year before and one year after the sale of the old residence.

Observation: If the replacement residence is constructed, the cost of the constructed residence would include: the cost of the land (including mortgage, if any), purchasing expenses and the costs of construction (including amount borrowed to finance construction). The cost of the land, however, counts only if it was acquired within two years before or after sale of the old residence. Costs of construction are treated as costs of the construction completed within this period.

Number of Deferrments Allowed

The law permits only one sale/replacement deferrement during a two year period, with one exception. Tax-deferred gain is allowed on the taxpayer's sale of more than one principal residence within the two year period where the second (or later) sale within the two year period was in connection with the commencement of work by the taxpayer as an employee or self-employed individual at a new principal place of work, and the second (or later) residence that he sells qualifies as a "former residence" under Code Section 217, which deals with deducting moving expenses, and the taxpayer also satisfies the distance and work requirements.

Time Limit for Buying or Building

The time limit for buying and moving into an already existing home is a time span of two years before or after the sale date of your old home. The time limit is the same whether you buy an existing home or decide to build a new one. You have from two years before to two years after the sale date of your prior residence to complete construction and occupy the new dwelling.

Illustration: Your home, bought several years ago, cost $65,000. You sell it for $140,000 and incur $5,000 in sales commissions and other expenses. For tax deferral purposes, you can buy a new home that costs at least $135,000 and you'll not be taxed on your gain of $70,000 ($135,000 minus $65,000.) The tax is deferred at least until you sell your new residence. You can keep putting off the tax on the profit if you replace each home you sell with a new home bought within the required period for a price at least equal to the selling price of the home sold. If you keep doing this till you reach the age of 55, you will become eligible for the once-in-a-lifetime exemption from income of up to $125,000 of any gain on the sale of your principal residence.

One-Time Exemption on Sale of Principal Residence

An individual, 55 or older, can exclude up to $125,000 in gain from the sale of his principal residence. To qualify, he must have owned and used the property as his principal residence for three of the five years just before the sale. This is a once-in-a-lifetime exclusion from income, and not just a tax deferral.

If a husband and wife own property as joint tenants, tenant by the entirety, or as community property, and file a joint return for the year of the sale, then only one of the spouses need satisfy the above age, holding period and use as principal residence requirements. Once a taxpayer or his or her spouse has made the election to exclude the gain from income, neither he nor she can make a similar election in later years with regards to their principal residence. The exclusion does not apply separately to each spouse. Thus, if husband and wife each owned separate homes prior to their marriage, and sold them subsequent to the marriage, only one of the homes would qualify for the exclusion, not both.

If a married couple gets divorced after making its one lifetime election to exclude, no further election would be available to either of them or to their new spouses if they get remarried.

Illustration: John and Mary, married to each other, sold their principal residence in January 1986. Having met the age, ownership and use test, they decide to exclude $100,000 of the gain on sale from their income in 1986. In 1987 John and Mary are divorced, and later in the same year, Mary marries Frank. Under a recommended strategy, if Frank owns a home in which he has lived for the last three of five years, and he is 55 or older in 1987, he should plan to sell his home prior to his marriage to Mary in order to exclude the gain on the sale from his income. Even though he later marries Mary who already has used up her exclusion, Frank would be allowed to claim the exclusion on their joint return for 1987.

If Frank waits to sell his home till after his marriage to Mary, the fact that Mary has already used up her once-in-a-lifetime exemption during her previous marriage will preclude Frank from claiming the exemption on his home.

Get the Maximum Out of the Exemption

There is yet another factor that should be taken into consideration by people who are eligible to claim the exclusion. Under the law, up to $125,000 of gain on sale can be excluded from the income. However, often the gain on sale of a particular residence would amount to only a small portion of this available exclusion. For example, if a 55-year old taxpayer elects to exclude $30,000 gain on sale of his present residence, he cannot again exclude a possibly larger gain on a future residence. He may do better by forgoing the available exclusion and reinvesting the proceeds of the sale into another residence within two years of the sale and rolling over the gain on the sale of the house. This way, there would be no taxable gain and he still would have available the one-shot exclusion for future use when it could be worth more.

Revocation of Election

The tax laws allow a taxpayer to make or revoke the election to exclude at any time within three years after the return is due for the year of sale. This gives him sufficient time to wait and see whether he is going to reinvest the sale proceeds into another residence and qualify for tax deferral under the rollover provisions or elect to exclude the gain.

A taxpayer may make or revoke a choice to exclude gain from a particular sale or exchange at any time before the latest of the following three dates: (a) three years from the due date of the return of the year of sale; (b) three years from the date the return was filed; (c) two years from the date the tax was paid. The election is made by attaching a statement to the return for the year the sale occurs. An election is revoked by filing a statement to that effect with the district director with whom the election was filed.

Spouses to Act Jointly

No married person can get the exclusion unless his or her spouse joins in the election. Taxpayer's spouse must join in the election even if the home is the separate property of either spouse, they file separate returns, or the spouse not owning an interest in the house had not lived in it for the required period before the sale or exchange. Similarly, a taxpayer who was married at the time of sale may not revoke the election unless his spouse joins in the revocation.

Illustration: John and Mary, both over age 55, planned to marry and to live in Mary's home. Before the wedding, John sold his residence and elected to avoid tax on the sale of his house. A few years later, John died and Mary sold her house and elected to avoid tax on the sale. The IRS allowed the election. Since John's sale was made before they married, his election did not affect her right to make an election after his death (Rev. Rul. 87-104, IRB 1987-43,12).

1. If John had not died and the couple had sold Mary's house, the election would have not been allowed. John's prior election would have barred Mary from making the election.

2. If John had sold his house after the marriage, rather than before, his election would have barred Mary from making the later election. Both spouses must consent to an election, and Mary's consent to John's election would have been considered an election on her part, barring her from making a later election.

Therefore, where a homeowner is considering marriage as well as sale of his or her house, the sale should occur before marriage to preserve a possible election for the other spouse as in the above case.

Glossary of Terms 18

Abstract of Title A summary of various ownership interests and liens and encumbrances placed on a real property. A title insurance company normally would trace this history of ownership and adverse claims against the property before insuring the title.

Acceleration Clause A mortgage loan agreement may stipulate that upon default of the borrower or sale of the property the entire loan balance shall be paid forthwith.

Adjustable Rate Mortgage In recent years this kind of mortgage has gained increasing acceptance among borrowers and is promoted heavily by lenders. Unlike the conventional fixed-rate mortgage, here the interest rate is adjusted periodically (every six months or a year) and moves up or down in conjunction with one of the widely-followed financial indexes. Such a mortgage enables a lender to match more closely its cost of acquiring funds with the return it can earn by lending them. The borrowers are enticed with a lower than normal initial interest rate and the prospect of lower monthly payments if the interest rates move downward.

Amortization A mortgage is amortized or paid off over a period of years by monthly payments that go toward reducing the principal and pay the interest on the borrowed sum.

Annual Percentage Rate (APR) This represents the cost of a loan converted to a yearly percentage. A true cost would also include the points and other fees paid for obtaining the loan.

Appraisal   A professional estimate of the market value of a property.

Appreciation   Increase in the value of a property over a period of time.

Assessed Value   Local city or county governments normally place a value on a property for taxing purposes. Generally this value only nominally reflects the current market value.

Assumable Mortgage   In an assumable mortgage a buyer may take over the existing financing on a property under its original terms and conditions. He may still have to qualify for the loan and pay the lender loan assumption fee.

Balloon Payment   Some loans are written so that the borrower is paying only the interest and only a small or no portion of principal during the term of the loan. Upon maturity the borrower is required to pay the entire unpaid balance of the principal in one lump sum plus any accrued interest. A fully amortized loan does not have a balloon payment.

You should be extremely wary of such loans because you may not have the large balance required at the end of the term of the loan. Such loans are typically of short duration and are meant to be a stop-gap financing tool.

Buy Down   A financing scheme in which the developer or seller of a real property typically reduces the interest rate charged on the loan by paying a portion of it himself. The lower interest rate not only attracts a larger number of prospective buyers but also makes it easier for them to qualify for the loan.

Cap Maximum interest rate that can be charged on a loan. Often a cap is mandated by state or federal laws. Many adjustable rate mortgages feature an interest rate cap beyond which the interest rate may not move.

Capital Gains Tax Tax on the profit derived from the sale of a capital asset, such as a home. Gain is calculated as the difference between the sale price of the asset and the cost basis after making appropriate adjustments for closing costs, capital improvements, allowable depreciation, etc.

Closing Costs These are expenses incurred in the course of acquiring a real property or refinancing a mortgage. Closing costs generally include loan origination fee, cost of appraisal, credit report, document preparation, filing and recording fees, title insurance premium and escrow fees. Closing costs may also include prorated taxes and insurance premiums. As a rule the escrow company or the attorney or another entity handling the closing of the transaction will render a closing statement upon the close of the escrow. Federal regulations also require that the buyer and seller be given a good faith estimate of the closing costs by the lender as soon as possible after the approval of the loan.

Cloud on Title An adverse outstanding claim or lien or encumbrance that may affect the marketability of the title to the real property. A title insurance company will generally not give a clear title report to a property if there is a cloud on the title.

Collateral Also known as security. Before a bank or lender will make a loan commitment, it would require a sufficient collateral guaranteeing the security of its money. House or land would generally be the collateral in a real estate financing. In the event of a default by the borrower the collateral may be seized by the lender and sold off to satisfy the loan.

Commission A real estate broker's commission for the sale and purchase of a real property. This commission is usually paid out of the proceeds of the sale and reduces the amount received by the seller.

In recent years there has been a definite trend toward negotiated commissions between the seller and broker. However, most transactions carry 6% commission on a residential property and 10% involving land. This commission is split between the seller's broker and buyer's broker.

Conventional Mortgage A mortgage not backed by a governmental agency such as VA or FHA. A borrower generally obtains a conventional mortgage from a private mortgage institution.

Conveyance The process of transfer of ownership or interest in a real property. When a note is fully paid back a full reconveyance takes place.

Counter Offer A typical real estate transaction may involve a series of offers and counter offers between a buyer and seller until either there is a meeting of the minds or the negotiations are broken off. A counter offer rejects or modifies the latest offer made by the other bargaining party. There usually is a time limit attached to an offer or a counter offer after which it is automatically withdrawn and becomes null and void.

Creative Financing A term that came into increasing vogue during the days of sky-high interest rates and tight supply of money to lend. It often denotes certain unconventional and invariably flexible means of financing employed to sell a property. The seller may carry a note with low interest rate with low monthly payments followed by a balloon payment - all done to accommodate a reluctant buyer.

Deed A legal document used to establish or transfer an interest in a real property.

Deed of Trust Some states use the term mortgage to denote the security interest in a real property. In a deed of trust there usually are three parties: borrower, lender and trustee. In such a transaction the borrower transfers the legal title to the property to the trustee to be held as collateral for the loan. When the loan is fully paid back to the lender the note and the deed of trust are canceled. In the event of a default of the borrower, the trustee upon instructions of the lender or beneficiary is empowered to sell the collateral (the real property) and convey the proceeds to the lender. In most jurisdictions that use the deed of trust the borrower is subject to having his property sold without the benefit of legal proceedings. The same states also allow the borrower to redeem the property by making the delinquent payments and reimbursing the trustee for his costs within a specified time.

Default This is a technical term used to describe the breaking of the conditions of the mortgage contract. Generally, when a mortgagor has been delinquent in his monthly payments for more than 30 days the mortgagee can at his option declare the loan to be in default, demand accelerated payment, obtain possession of the property and start foreclosure proceedings. In most cases a default can be cured by prompt and corrective action by the mortgagor. Default may also come about by a breach of other conditions of the mortgage or deed of trust.

Depreciation A real property is depreciated over a period of years using its cost basis value. The method used for computing depreciation may be a straight-line method, double declining method or one of the other generally accepted methods. Depreciation allows a certain sum to be set aside each year to account for the gradual wear and tear of the property and eventual replacement. Land is never depreciated.

Down Payment   A purchaser of a real property is required to make a down payment in the amount that is the difference between the purchase price and mortgage incurred. Upon purchase the down payment signifies the buyer's equity in the property.

Due on Sale   Many mortgage contracts contain a due on sale clause giving the lender the right to call the entire balance of the mortgage as due and payable in the event the property is sold. Many other types of loans are assumable by the new owners if they qualify.

Earnest Money Deposit   In a real property transaction a purchaser is required to put down a certain sum of money as good faith deposit which is ultimately applied to the purchase price. Generally, this money would be refunded to the buyer if he fails to qualify for the necessary financing or if the transaction cannot be completed for no fault of his. However, if he reneges on the transaction, depending upon the exact language of the contract, he may forfeit to the seller the earnest money deposit as liquidated damages.

Easement   A right granted by a property owner to someone to use a portion of the property for a specific purpose.

Encumbrance   A legal right or claim affecting the ownership interest in a real property. An encumbrance clouds the title to the property, reduces its marketability and diminishes its sale value. It can take numerous forms, such as mortgages, liens, unpaid taxes, pending legal action, zoning ordinances, easement rights, or restrictive covenants. A diligent title search by a title insurance company will uncover any encumbrances placed on the property. A buyer should complete the transaction only after ensuring that all encumbrances are removed and that he is receiving a good and clear title.

Equity This represents a homeowner's interest in a real property. It is computed by subtracting from the fair market value of the property any unpaid mortgages and outstanding liens or debts against the property. Homeowner's equity will increase as the mortgage is paid down or as the property appreciates in market value.

Escrow A real property transaction is almost always handled through an escrow agent. The purpose of escrow is to ensure that buyer and seller have fulfilled their individual obligations prior to the transfer of title and money.

Fixed Rate Mortgage A mortgage that charges a fixed rate of interest throughout the term of the loan. Compare this with an adjustable rate mortgage.

Foreclosure When the borrower has defaulted on the terms of his loan, the lender may initiate foreclosure proceedings by taking possession of the security and forcing its sale.

Junior Lien A lien recorded subsequent to another lien. A junior lien holds a lower priority than a senior and would be paid only after all senior liens have been satisfied.

Leasehold Interest The right to use a property under certain conditions but it does not include the right of ownership.

Lease with Option to Buy A landlord may rent or lease a property to a tenant and grant him an option to purchase the property within a specified time in the future under certain conditions.

Lien   This is a legal claim placed against a property to ensure payment of a debt.   A creditor may place a judgment lien, a taxing authority may place a tax lien and unpaid contractors and mechanics may place a mechanic's lien until their debts are paid by the homeowner.   A lien creates a cloud on the title and would normally require them to be cleared before the property can be sold.

Loan Origination Fee   This is a fee charged by a bank or financial institution at the time of making the loan and is usually represented as points or percentage of the amount borrowed. Technically this is interest prepaid and the IRS allows the loan origination fee to be a deductible expense if it is amortized over the life of the loan.

Mortgage   A buyer is required to provide security or collateral for the loan to the lender.   Mortgage is a claim or lien against the real property given by the buyer to the lender as security for payment of the loan.

Mortgage Insurance Premium   FHA and sometimes private lenders require a mortgagor to buy mortgage insurance under certain circumstances.   For instance, when a borrower is able to put less than the normal down payment while purchasing a property, the lender may require additional security in the form of a private mortgage insurance.   This is an additional cost to the borrower and should be resisted whenever possible.

Mortgagee   The bank or lender who lends the money to the borrower for the purchase of a real property. The mortgagee holds the note till the debt is paid back.

Mortgagor   The borrower of the money who provides the collateral to the lender to secure payment of the debt.

PI Principal and interest portion of a monthly mortgage payment.

PITI Principal, interest, real property taxes and insurance that comprise a monthly mortgage payment. If a lender requires an impound account, he would collect on a monthly basis taxes and insurance and would make a direct payment when they are due.

Points Points are a percent of the loan amount charged by the lender to increase his yield. A point is one percent of the amount of the mortgage loan. Competitive conditions, money supply and borrower's credit worthiness will determine the number of points demanded by the lender. For instance, a non-owner occupied property purchase would command a slightly higher interest rate and higher than normal points from the lender.

Prepayment Penalty Prepayment of a mortgage (or portions of a mortgage) before its due date may trigger a prepayment penalty from the lender. Many mortgages contain no prepayment penalty. FHA insured mortgages cannot have any restrictions on prepaying the mortgage. Even the lenders who do impose a prepayment penalty generally allow a certain amount to be prepaid every year without incurring any penalty.

Principal This is the amount of the loan. Interest is charged on the principal amount of the loan.

Purchase Offer An offer made to purchase a real estate by a potential buyer. This is a legally binding contract and would contain terms and conditions of the offer and any other contingencies. It is usually accompanied with a good faith deposit which, if the offer is accepted, would be applied toward the purchase price.

Recording Fee A fee charged by the county or city recorder's office for recording a document. Grant deeds, liens, default notices, abstracts of judgments, etc. are recorded in a local office where land records are maintained.

Refinancing Refinancing occurs when a mortgagor pays off an existing mortgage with the proceeds of another loan. If the current mortgage was obtained at a higher interest rate than presently available, a homeowner may wish to refinance the property at a lower interest rate and lower his monthly payments and total interest costs. Refinancing has its own costs too, such as loan origination fee and other closing costs.

Secondary Market Various governmental agencies such as Federal Home Loan Bank, Federal National Mortgage Association, etc. routinely buy mortgages written by private lenders and repackage them for sale on the open market which is known as secondary market. This brings added liquidity to the mortgage market by making more money available for lending.

Second Mortgage or Second Deed of Trust A junior mortgage or lien placed on a real property. Such a mortgage is additional financing obtained by the property owner usually at a higher interest rate for a shorter period of time. Second mortgage would occupy a junior position vis-a-vis first mortgage in the event of a default.

Security Same as collateral. Lenders require a borrower to put up a security to ensure that a loan will be repaid. In the event of a default, the security is seized and sold to pay off the loan.

Shared Appreciation Mortgage This is one of the many innovative mortgages that have been marketed from time to time by various lenders. In a shared appreciation mortgage, the lender offers a lower than market interest rate or some other concession in return for the right to participate in the appreciation enjoyed by the real property. Not too many banks or financial institutions offer such a mortgage, and you would have to look around hard to find one if you were interested in it.

Title   Legal document that establishes the right of ownership in a real property.

Title Insurance Policy   This is an insurance policy issued by a title insurance company guaranteeing a lender or a borrower that the title is good and clear, that there are no clouds or claims against it. The policy obligates the title insurance company to defend the title against any adverse claims or liens of third parties.

Title Search   A tracing of the title to a real property through public records to verify that the owner does own the property and has a right to sell it.

Wraparound Mortgage   Another innovative device to expedite the sale of a property. A seller offers to carry a wraparound mortgage in which part of the financing is created by the seller who collects the payments from the buyer and forwards applicable portions to the other underlying mortgagees. This relieves the buyer from having to look for new financing which may be hard to come by or may be too costly.

8% MONTHLY PAYMENT
necessary to amortize a loan

AMOUNT	1 YEAR	3 YEARS	5 YEARS	8 YEARS	10 YEARS
$ 50	4.35	1.57	1.02	.71	.61
100	8.70	3.14	2.03	1.42	1.22
200	17.40	6.27	4.06	2.83	2.43
300	26.10	9.41	6.09	4.25	3.64
400	34.80	12.54	8.12	5.66	4.86
500	43.50	15.67	10.14	7.07	6.07
600	52.20	18.81	12.17	8.49	7.28
700	60.90	21.94	14.20	9.90	8.50
800	69.60	25.07	16.23	11.31	9.71
900	78.29	28.21	18.25	12.73	10.92
1000	86.99	31.34	20.28	14.14	12.14
2000	173.98	62.68	40.56	28.28	24.27
3000	260.97	94.01	60.83	42.42	36.40
4000	347.96	125.35	81.11	56.55	48.54
5000	434.95	156.69	101.39	70.69	60.67
6000	521.94	188.02	121.66	84.83	72.80
7000	608.92	219.36	141.94	98.96	84.93
8000	695.91	250.70	162.22	113.10	97.07
9000	782.90	282.03	182.49	127.24	109.20
10000	869.89	313.37	202.77	141.37	121.33
15000	1304.83	470.05	304.15	212.06	182.00
20000	1739.77	626.73	405.53	282.74	242.66
25000	2174.72	783.41	506.91	353.42	303.32
30000	2609.66	940.10	608.30	424.11	363.99
35000	3044.60	1096.78	709.68	494.79	424.65
40000	3479.54	1253.46	811.06	565.47	485.32
45000	3914.48	1410.14	912.44	636.16	545.98
46000	4001.47	1441.48	932.72	650.29	558.11
47000	4088.46	1472.81	953.00	664.43	570.24
48000	4175.45	1504.15	973.27	678.57	582.38
49000	4262.44	1535.49	993.55	692.70	594.51
50000	4349.43	1566.82	1013.82	706.84	606.64
51000	4436.41	1598.16	1034.10	720.98	618.78
52000	4523.40	1629.50	1054.38	735.11	630.91
53000	4610.39	1660.83	1074.65	749.25	643.04
54000	4697.38	1692.17	1094.93	763.39	655.17
55000	4784.37	1723.51	1115.21	777.52	667.31
56000	4871.36	1754.84	1135.48	791.66	679.44
57000	4958.35	1786.18	1155.76	805.80	691.57
58000	5045.33	1817.51	1176.04	819.93	703.71
59000	5132.32	1848.85	1196.31	834.07	715.84
60000	5219.31	1880.19	1216.59	848.21	727.97
61000	5306.30	1911.52	1236.87	862.34	740.10
62000	5393.29	1942.86	1257.14	876.48	752.24
63000	5480.28	1974.20	1277.42	890.62	764.37
64000	5567.26	2005.53	1297.69	904.75	776.50
65000	5654.25	2036.87	1317.97	918.89	788.63
67500	5871.72	2115.21	1368.66	954.23	818.97
70000	6089.20	2193.55	1419.35	989.57	849.30
75000	6524.14	2350.23	1520.73	1060.26	909.96
80000	6959.08	2506.91	1622.12	1130.94	970.63
85000	7394.02	2663.60	1723.50	1201.62	1031.29
90000	7828.96	2820.28	1824.88	1272.31	1091.95
95000	8263.91	2976.96	1926.26	1342.99	1152.62
100000	8698.85	3133.64	2027.64	1413.67	1213.28
105000	9133.79	3290.32	2129.03	1484.36	1273.94
110000	9568.73	3447.01	2230.41	1555.04	1334.61
115000	10003.67	3603.69	2331.79	1625.72	1395.27
120000	10438.62	3760.37	2433.17	1696.41	1455.94
125000	10873.56	3917.05	2534.55	1767.09	1516.60
130000	11308.50	4073.73	2635.94	1837.77	1577.26
135000	11743.44	4230.41	2737.32	1908.46	1637.93
140000	12178.39	4387.10	2838.70	1979.14	1698.59
145000	12613.33	4543.78	2940.08	2049.82	1759.26
150000	13048.27	4700.46	3041.46	2120.51	1819.92

MONTHLY PAYMENT
necessary to amortize a loan
8%

AMOUNT	12 YEARS	15 YEARS	20 YEARS	25 YEARS	30 YEARS
$ 50	.55	.48	.42	.39	.37
100	1.09	.96	.84	.78	.74
200	2.17	1.92	1.68	1.55	1.47
300	3.25	2.87	2.51	2.32	2.21
400	4.33	3.83	3.35	3.09	2.94
500	5.42	4.78	4.19	3.86	3.67
600	6.50	5.74	5.02	4.64	4.41
700	7.58	6.69	5.86	5.41	5.14
800	8.66	7.65	6.70	6.18	5.88
900	9.75	8.61	7.53	6.95	6.61
1000	10.83	9.56	8.37	7.72	7.34
2000	21.65	19.12	16.73	15.44	14.68
3000	32.48	28.67	25.10	23.16	22.02
4000	43.30	38.23	33.46	30.88	29.36
5000	54.13	47.79	41.83	38.60	36.69
6000	64.95	57.34	50.19	46.31	44.03
7000	75.78	66.90	58.56	54.03	51.37
8000	86.60	76.46	66.92	61.75	58.71
9000	97.43	86.01	75.28	69.47	66.04
10000	108.25	95.57	83.65	77.19	73.38
15000	162.37	143.35	125.47	115.78	110.07
20000	216.50	191.14	167.29	154.37	146.76
25000	270.62	238.92	209.12	192.96	183.45
30000	324.74	286.70	250.94	231.55	220.13
35000	378.86	334.48	292.76	270.14	256.82
40000	432.99	382.27	334.58	308.73	293.51
45000	487.11	430.05	376.40	347.32	330.20
46000	497.93	439.60	384.77	355.04	337.54
47000	508.76	449.16	393.13	362.76	344.87
48000	519.58	458.72	401.50	370.48	352.21
49000	530.41	468.27	409.86	378.19	359.55
50000	541.23	477.83	418.23	385.91	366.89
51000	552.06	487.39	426.59	393.63	374.22
52000	562.88	496.94	434.95	401.35	381.56
53000	573.70	506.50	443.32	409.07	388.90
54000	584.53	516.06	451.68	416.79	396.24
55000	595.35	525.61	460.05	424.50	403.58
56000	606.18	535.17	468.41	432.22	410.91
57000	617.00	544.73	476.78	439.94	418.25
58000	627.83	554.28	485.14	447.66	425.59
59000	638.65	563.84	493.50	455.38	432.93
60000	649.48	573.40	501.87	463.09	440.26
61000	660.30	582.95	510.23	470.81	447.60
62000	671.13	592.51	518.60	478.53	454.94
63000	681.95	602.07	526.96	486.25	462.28
64000	692.77	611.62	535.33	493.97	469.61
65000	703.60	621.18	543.69	501.69	476.95
67500	730.66	645.07	564.60	520.98	495.30
70000	757.72	668.96	585.51	540.28	513.64
75000	811.84	716.74	627.34	578.87	550.33
80000	865.97	764.53	669.16	617.46	587.02
85000	920.09	812.31	710.98	656.05	623.70
90000	974.21	860.09	752.80	694.64	660.39
95000	1028.33	907.87	794.62	733.23	697.08
100000	1082.46	955.66	836.45	771.82	733.77
105000	1136.58	1003.44	878.27	810.41	770.46
110000	1190.70	1051.22	920.09	849.00	807.15
115000	1244.83	1099.00	961.91	887.59	843.83
120000	1298.95	1146.79	1003.73	926.18	880.52
125000	1353.07	1194.57	1045.56	964.78	917.21
130000	1407.19	1242.35	1087.38	1003.37	953.90
135000	1461.32	1290.14	1129.20	1041.96	990.59
140000	1515.44	1337.92	1171.02	1080.55	1027.28
145000	1569.56	1385.70	1212.84	1119.14	1063.96
150000	1623.68	1433.48	1254.67	1157.73	1100.65

8.5%
MONTHLY PAYMENT
necessary to amortize a loan

AMOUNT	1 YEAR	3 YEARS	5 YEARS	8 YEARS	10 YEARS
$ 50	4.37	1.58	1.03	.72	.62
100	8.73	3.16	2.06	1.44	1.24
200	17.45	6.32	4.11	2.88	2.48
300	26.17	9.48	6.16	4.32	3.72
400	34.89	12.63	8.21	5.76	4.96
500	43.61	15.79	10.26	7.20	6.20
600	52.34	18.95	12.31	8.64	7.44
700	61.06	22.10	14.37	10.08	8.68
800	69.78	25.26	16.42	11.52	9.92
900	78.50	28.42	18.47	12.96	11.16
1000	87.22	31.57	20.52	14.40	12.40
2000	174.44	63.14	41.04	28.79	24.80
3000	261.66	94.71	61.55	43.18	37.20
4000	348.88	126.28	82.07	57.57	49.60
5000	436.10	157.84	102.59	71.97	62.00
6000	523.32	189.41	123.10	86.36	74.40
7000	610.54	220.98	143.62	100.75	86.79
8000	697.76	252.55	164.14	115.14	99.19
9000	784.98	284.11	184.65	129.53	111.59
10000	872.20	315.68	205.17	143.93	123.99
15000	1308.30	473.52	307.75	215.89	185.98
20000	1744.40	631.36	410.34	287.85	247.98
25000	2180.50	789.19	512.92	359.81	309.97
30000	2616.60	947.03	615.50	431.77	371.96
35000	3052.70	1104.87	718.08	503.73	433.95
40000	3488.80	1262.71	820.67	575.69	495.95
45000	3924.90	1420.54	923.25	647.65	557.94
46000	4012.11	1452.11	943.77	662.04	570.34
47000	4099.33	1483.68	964.28	676.44	582.74
48000	4186.55	1515.25	984.80	690.83	595.14
49000	4273.77	1546.81	1005.32	705.22	607.53
50000	4360.99	1578.38	1025.83	719.61	619.93
51000	4448.21	1609.95	1046.35	734.00	632.33
52000	4535.43	1641.52	1066.86	748.40	644.73
53000	4622.65	1673.08	1087.38	762.79	657.13
54000	4709.87	1704.65	1107.90	777.18	669.53
55000	4797.09	1736.22	1128.41	791.57	681.93
56000	4884.31	1767.79	1148.93	805.96	694.32
57000	4971.53	1799.35	1169.45	820.36	706.72
58000	5058.75	1830.92	1189.96	834.75	719.12
59000	5145.97	1862.49	1210.48	849.14	731.52
60000	5233.19	1894.06	1231.00	863.53	743.92
61000	5320.41	1925.62	1251.51	877.92	756.32
62000	5407.63	1957.19	1272.03	892.32	768.72
63000	5494.85	1988.76	1292.55	906.71	781.11
64000	5582.07	2020.33	1313.06	921.10	793.51
65000	5669.29	2051.89	1333.58	935.49	805.91
67500	5887.34	2130.81	1384.87	971.47	836.91
70000	6105.39	2209.73	1436.16	1007.45	867.90
75000	6541.49	2367.57	1538.74	1079.41	929.90
80000	6977.59	2525.41	1641.33	1151.38	991.89
85000	7413.69	2683.25	1743.91	1223.34	1053.88
90000	7849.79	2841.08	1846.49	1295.30	1115.88
95000	8285.88	2998.92	1949.08	1367.26	1177.87
100000	8721.98	3156.76	2051.66	1439.22	1239.86
105000	9158.08	3314.60	2154.24	1511.18	1301.85
110000	9594.18	3472.43	2256.82	1583.14	1363.85
115000	10030.28	3630.27	2359.41	1655.10	1425.84
120000	10466.38	3788.11	2461.99	1727.06	1487.83
125000	10902.48	3945.95	2564.57	1799.02	1549.83
130000	11338.58	4103.78	2667.15	1870.98	1611.82
135000	11774.68	4261.62	2769.74	1942.94	1673.81
140000	12210.77	4419.46	2872.32	2014.90	1735.80
145000	12646.87	4577.30	2974.90	2086.86	1797.80
150000	13082.97	4735.14	3077.48	2158.82	1859.79

MONTHLY PAYMENT 8.5%
necessary to amortize a loan

AMOUNT	12 YEARS	15 YEARS	20 YEARS	25 YEARS	30 YEARS
$ 50	.56	.50	.47	.41	.39
100	1.12	.99	.87	.81	.77
200	2.23	1.97	1.74	1.62	1.54
300	3.34	2.96	2.61	2.42	2.31
400	4.45	3.94	3.48	3.23	3.08
500	5.56	4.93	4.34	4.03	3.85
600	6.67	5.91	5.21	4.84	4.62
700	7.78	6.90	6.08	5.64	5.39
800	8.89	7.88	6.95	6.45	6.16
900	10.00	8.87	7.82	7.25	6.93
1000	11.11	9.85	8.68	8.06	7.69
2000	22.21	19.70	17.36	16.11	15.38
3000	33.31	29.55	26.04	24.16	23.07
4000	44.41	39.39	34.72	32.21	30.76
5000	55.51	49.24	43.40	40.27	38.45
6000	66.61	59.09	52.07	48.32	46.14
7000	77.71	68.94	60.75	56.37	53.83
8000	88.81	78.78	69.43	64.42	61.52
9000	99.91	88.63	78.11	72.48	69.21
10000	111.01	98.48	86.79	80.53	76.90
15000	166.51	147.72	130.18	120.79	115.34
20000	222.02	196.95	173.57	161.05	153.79
25000	277.52	246.19	216.96	201.31	192.23
30000	333.02	295.43	260.35	241.57	230.68
35000	388.52	344.66	303.74	281.83	269.12
40000	444.03	393.90	347.13	322.10	307.57
45000	499.53	443.14	390.53	362.36	346.02
46000	510.63	452.99	399.20	370.41	353.71
47000	521.73	462.83	407.88	378.46	361.39
48000	532.83	472.68	416.56	386.51	369.08
49000	543.93	482.53	425.24	394.57	376.77
50000	555.03	492.37	433.92	402.62	384.46
51000	566.13	502.22	442.59	410.67	392.15
52000	577.23	512.07	451.27	418.72	399.84
53000	588.33	521.92	459.95	426.78	407.53
54000	599.44	531.76	468.63	434.83	415.22
55000	610.54	541.61	477.31	442.88	422.91
56000	621.64	551.46	485.99	450.93	430.60
57000	632.74	561.31	494.66	458.98	438.29
58000	643.84	571.15	503.34	467.04	445.97
59000	654.94	581.00	512.02	475.09	453.66
60000	666.04	590.85	520.70	483.14	461.35
61000	677.14	600.70	529.38	491.19	469.04
62000	688.24	610.54	538.06	499.25	476.73
63000	699.34	620.39	546.73	507.30	484.42
64000	710.44	630.24	555.41	515.35	492.11
65000	721.54	640.09	564.09	523.40	499.80
67500	749.29	664.70	585.79	543.53	519.02
70000	777.04	689.32	607.48	563.66	538.24
75000	832.55	738.56	650.87	603.93	576.69
80000	888.05	787.80	694.26	644.19	615.14
85000	943.55	837.03	737.65	684.45	653.58
90000	999.06	886.27	781.05	724.71	692.03
95000	1054.56	935.51	824.44	764.97	730.47
100000	1110.06	984.74	867.83	805.23	768.92
105000	1165.56	1033.98	911.22	845.49	807.36
110000	1221.07	1083.22	954.61	885.75	845.81
115000	1276.57	1132.46	998.00	926.02	884.26
120000	1332.07	1181.69	1041.39	966.28	922.70
125000	1387.57	1230.93	1084.78	1006.54	961.15
130000	1443.08	1280.17	1128.18	1046.80	999.59
135000	1498.58	1329.40	1171.57	1087.06	1038.04
140000	1554.08	1378.64	1214.96	1127.32	1076.48
145000	1609.59	1427.88	1258.35	1167.58	1114.93
150000	1665.09	1477.11	1301.74	1207.85	1153.38

9%
MONTHLY PAYMENT
necessary to amortize a loan

AMOUNT	1 YEAR	3 YEARS	5 YEARS	8 YEARS	10 YEARS
$ 50	4.38	1.59	1.04	.74	.64
100	8.75	3.18	2.08	1.47	1.27
200	17.50	6.36	4.16	2.94	2.54
300	26.24	9.54	6.23	4.40	3.81
400	34.99	12.72	8.31	5.87	5.07
500	43.73	15.90	10.38	7.33	6.34
600	52.48	19.08	12.46	8.80	7.61
700	61.22	22.26	14.54	10.26	8.87
800	69.97	25.44	16.61	11.73	10.14
900	78.71	28.62	18.69	13.19	11.41
1000	87.46	31.80	20.76	14.66	12.67
2000	174.91	63.60	41.52	29.31	25.34
3000	262.36	95.40	62.28	43.96	38.01
4000	349.81	127.20	83.04	58.61	50.68
5000	437.26	159.00	103.80	73.26	63.34
6000	524.71	190.80	124.56	87.91	76.01
7000	612.17	222.60	145.31	102.56	88.68
8000	699.62	254.40	166.07	117.21	101.35
9000	787.07	286.20	186.83	131.86	114.01
10000	874.52	318.00	207.59	146.51	126.68
15000	1311.78	477.00	311.38	219.76	190.02
20000	1749.03	636.00	415.17	293.01	253.36
25000	2186.29	795.00	518.96	366.26	316.69
30000	2623.55	954.00	622.76	439.51	380.03
35000	3060.81	1113.00	726.55	512.76	443.37
40000	3498.06	1271.99	830.34	586.01	506.71
45000	3935.32	1430.99	934.13	659.26	570.05
46000	4022.77	1462.79	954.89	673.91	582.71
47000	4110.22	1494.59	975.65	688.56	595.38
48000	4197.68	1526.39	996.41	703.21	608.05
49000	4285.13	1558.19	1017.16	717.86	620.72
50000	4372.58	1589.99	1037.92	732.52	633.38
51000	4460.03	1621.79	1058.68	747.17	646.05
52000	4547.48	1653.59	1079.44	761.82	658.72
53000	4634.93	1685.39	1100.20	776.47	671.39
54000	4722.38	1717.19	1120.96	791.12	684.05
55000	4809.84	1748.99	1141.71	805.77	696.72
56000	4897.29	1780.79	1162.47	820.42	709.39
57000	4984.74	1812.59	1183.23	835.07	722.06
58000	5072.19	1844.39	1203.99	849.72	734.72
59000	5159.64	1876.19	1224.75	864.37	747.39
60000	5247.09	1907.99	1245.51	879.02	760.06
61000	5334.55	1939.79	1266.26	893.67	772.73
62000	5422.00	1971.59	1287.02	908.32	785.39
63000	5509.45	2003.39	1307.78	922.97	798.06
64000	5596.90	2035.19	1328.54	937.62	810.73
65000	5684.35	2066.99	1349.30	952.27	823.40
67500	5902.98	2146.49	1401.19	988.89	855.07
70000	6121.61	2225.99	1453.09	1025.52	886.74
75000	6558.87	2384.98	1556.88	1098.77	950.07
80000	6996.12	2543.98	1660.67	1172.02	1013.41
85000	7433.38	2702.98	1764.47	1245.27	1076.75
90000	7870.64	2861.98	1868.26	1318.52	1140.09
95000	8307.90	3020.98	1972.05	1391.77	1203.42
100000	8745.15	3179.98	2075.84	1465.03	1266.76
105000	9182.41	3338.98	2179.63	1538.28	1330.10
110000	9619.67	3497.98	2283.42	1611.53	1393.44
115000	10056.92	3656.97	2387.22	1684.78	1456.78
120000	10494.18	3815.97	2491.01	1758.03	1520.11
125000	10931.44	3974.97	2594.80	1831.28	1583.45
130000	11368.70	4133.97	2698.59	1904.53	1646.79
135000	11805.95	4292.97	2802.38	1977.78	1710.13
140000	12243.21	4451.97	2906.17	2051.03	1773.47
145000	12680.47	4610.97	3009.97	2124.28	1836.80
150000	13117.73	4769.96	3113.76	2197.54	1900.14

MONTHLY PAYMENT
necessary to amortize a loan
9%

AMOUNT	12 YEARS	15 YEARS	20 YEARS	25 YEARS	30 YEARS
$ 50	.57	.51	.45	.42	.41
100	1.14	1.02	.90	.84	.81
200	2.28	2.03	1.80	1.68	1.61
300	3.42	3.05	2.70	2.52	2.42
400	4.56	4.06	3.60	3.36	3.22
500	5.70	5.08	4.50	4.20	4.03
600	6.83	6.09	5.40	5.04	4.83
700	7.97	7.10	6.30	5.88	5.64
800	9.11	8.12	7.20	6.72	6.44
900	10.25	9.13	8.10	7.56	7.25
1000	11.39	10.15	9.00	8.40	8.05
2000	22.77	20.29	18.00	16.79	16.10
3000	34.15	30.43	27.00	25.18	24.14
4000	45.53	40.58	35.99	33.57	32.19
5000	56.91	50.72	44.99	41.96	40.24
6000	68.29	60.86	53.99	50.36	48.28
7000	79.67	71.00	62.99	58.75	56.33
8000	91.05	81.15	71.98	67.14	64.37
9000	102.43	91.29	80.98	75.53	72.42
10000	113.81	101.43	89.98	83.92	80.47
15000	170.71	152.14	134.96	125.88	120.70
20000	227.61	202.86	179.95	167.84	160.93
25000	284.51	253.57	224.94	209.80	201.16
30000	341.41	304.28	269.92	251.76	241.39
35000	398.32	355.00	314.91	293.72	281.62
40000	455.22	405.71	359.90	335.68	321.85
45000	512.12	456.42	404.88	377.64	362.09
46000	523.50	466.57	413.88	386.04	370.13
47000	534.88	476.71	422.88	394.43	378.18
48000	546.26	486.85	431.87	402.82	386.22
49000	557.64	497.00	440.87	411.21	394.27
50000	569.02	507.14	449.87	419.60	402.32
51000	580.40	517.28	458.87	428.00	410.36
52000	591.78	527.42	467.86	436.39	418.41
53000	603.16	537.57	476.86	444.78	426.45
54000	614.54	547.71	485.86	453.17	434.50
55000	625.92	557.85	494.85	461.56	442.55
56000	637.30	567.99	503.85	469.95	450.59
57000	648.68	578.14	512.85	478.35	458.64
58000	660.06	588.28	521.85	486.74	466.69
59000	671.44	598.42	530.84	495.13	474.73
60000	682.82	608.56	539.84	503.52	482.78
61000	694.20	618.71	548.84	511.91	490.82
62000	705.58	628.85	557.84	520.31	498.87
63000	716.96	638.99	566.83	528.70	506.92
64000	728.34	649.14	575.83	537.09	514.96
65000	739.72	659.28	584.83	545.48	523.01
67500	768.18	684.63	607.32	566.46	543.13
70000	796.63	709.99	629.81	587.44	563.24
75000	853.53	760.70	674.80	629.40	603.47
80000	910.43	811.42	719.79	671.36	643.70
85000	967.33	862.13	764.77	713.32	683.93
90000	1024.23	912.84	809.76	755.28	724.17
95000	1081.13	963.56	854.74	797.24	764.40
100000	1138.04	1014.27	899.73	839.20	804.63
105000	1194.94	1064.98	944.72	881.16	844.86
110000	1251.84	1115.70	989.70	923.12	885.09
115000	1308.74	1166.41	1034.69	965.08	925.32
120000	1365.64	1217.12	1079.68	1007.04	965.55
125000	1422.54	1267.84	1124.66	1049.00	1005.78
130000	1479.44	1318.55	1169.65	1090.96	1046.01
135000	1536.35	1369.26	1214.64	1132.92	1086.25
140000	1593.25	1419.98	1259.62	1174.88	1126.48
145000	1650.15	1470.69	1304.61	1216.84	1166.71
150000	1707.05	1521.40	1349.59	1258.80	1206.94

9.5% MONTHLY PAYMENT
necessary to amortize a loan

AMOUNT	1 YEAR	3 YEARS	5 YEARS	8 YEARS	10 YEARS
$ 50	4.39	1.61	1.06	.75	.65
100	8.77	3.21	2.11	1.50	1.30
200	17.54	6.41	4.21	2.99	2.59
300	26.31	9.61	6.31	4.48	3.89
400	35.08	12.82	8.41	5.97	5.18
500	43.85	16.02	10.51	7.46	6.47
600	52.62	19.22	12.61	8.95	7.77
700	61.38	22.43	14.71	10.44	9.06
800	70.15	25.63	16.81	11.93	10.36
900	78.92	28.83	18.91	13.42	11.65
1000	87.69	32.04	21.01	14.92	12.94
2000	175.37	64.07	42.01	29.83	25.88
3000	263.06	96.10	63.01	44.74	38.82
4000	350.74	128.14	84.01	59.65	51.76
5000	438.42	160.17	105.01	74.56	64.70
6000	526.11	192.20	126.02	89.47	77.64
7000	613.79	224.24	147.02	104.38	90.58
8000	701.47	256.27	168.02	119.29	103.52
9000	789.16	288.30	189.02	134.20	116.46
10000	876.84	320.33	210.02	149.11	129.40
15000	1315.26	480.50	315.03	223.67	194.10
20000	1753.68	640.66	420.04	298.22	258.80
25000	2192.09	800.83	525.05	372.78	323.50
30000	2630.51	960.99	630.06	447.33	388.20
35000	3068.93	1121.16	735.07	521.89	452.90
40000	3507.35	1281.32	840.08	596.44	517.60
45000	3945.76	1441.49	945.09	670.99	582.29
46000	4033.45	1473.52	966.09	685.91	595.23
47000	4121.13	1505.55	987.09	700.82	608.17
48000	4208.81	1537.59	1008.09	715.73	621.11
49000	4296.50	1569.62	1029.10	730.64	634.05
50000	4384.18	1601.65	1050.10	745.55	646.99
51000	4471.86	1633.69	1071.10	760.46	659.93
52000	4559.55	1665.72	1092.10	775.37	672.87
53000	4647.23	1697.75	1113.10	790.28	685.81
54000	4734.91	1729.78	1134.11	805.19	698.75
55000	4822.60	1761.82	1155.11	820.10	711.69
56000	4910.28	1793.85	1176.11	835.01	724.63
57000	4997.97	1825.88	1197.11	849.93	737.57
58000	5085.65	1857.92	1218.11	864.84	750.51
59000	5173.33	1889.95	1239.11	879.75	763.45
60000	5261.02	1921.98	1260.12	894.66	776.39
61000	5348.70	1954.01	1281.12	909.57	789.33
62000	5436.38	1986.05	1302.12	924.48	802.27
63000	5524.07	2018.08	1323.12	939.39	815.21
64000	5611.75	2050.11	1344.12	954.30	828.15
65000	5699.43	2082.15	1365.13	969.21	841.09
67500	5918.64	2162.23	1417.63	1006.49	873.44
70000	6137.85	2242.31	1470.14	1043.77	905.79
75000	6576.27	2402.48	1575.14	1118.32	970.49
80000	7014.69	2562.64	1680.15	1192.88	1035.19
85000	7453.10	2722.81	1785.16	1267.43	1099.88
90000	7891.52	2882.97	1890.17	1341.98	1164.58
95000	8329.94	3043.14	1995.18	1416.54	1229.28
100000	8768.36	3203.30	2100.19	1491.09	1293.98
105000	9206.77	3363.46	2205.20	1565.65	1358.68
110000	9645.19	3523.63	2310.21	1640.20	1423.38
115000	10083.61	3683.79	2415.22	1714.76	1488.08
120000	10522.03	3843.96	2520.23	1789.31	1552.78
125000	10960.44	4004.12	2625.24	1863.87	1617.47
130000	11398.86	4164.29	2730.25	1938.42	1682.17
135000	11837.28	4324.45	2835.26	2012.97	1746.87
140000	12275.70	4484.62	2940.27	2087.53	1811.57
145000	12714.11	4644.78	3045.27	2162.08	1876.27
150000	13152.53	4804.95	3150.28	2236.64	1940.97

MONTHLY PAYMENT
necessary to amortize a loan

9.5%

AMOUNT	12 YEARS	15 YEARS	20 YEARS	25 YEARS	30 YEARS
$ 50	.59	.53	.47	.44	.43
100	1.17	1.05	.94	.88	.85
200	2.34	2.09	1.87	1.75	1.69
300	3.50	3.14	2.80	2.63	2.53
400	4.67	4.18	3.73	3.50	3.37
500	5.84	5.23	4.67	4.37	4.21
600	7.00	6.27	5.60	5.25	5.05
700	8.17	7.31	6.53	6.12	5.89
800	9.34	8.36	7.46	6.99	6.73
900	10.50	9.40	8.39	7.87	7.57
1000	11.67	10.45	9.33	8.74	8.41
2000	23.33	20.89	18.65	17.48	16.82
3000	35.00	31.33	27.97	26.22	25.23
4000	46.66	41.77	37.29	34.95	33.64
5000	58.32	52.22	46.61	43.69	42.05
6000	69.99	62.66	55.93	52.43	50.46
7000	81.65	73.10	65.25	61.16	58.86
8000	93.31	83.54	74.58	69.90	67.27
9000	104.98	93.99	83.90	78.64	75.68
10000	116.64	104.43	93.22	87.37	84.09
15000	174.96	156.64	139.82	131.06	126.13
20000	233.28	208.85	186.43	174.74	168.18
25000	291.60	261.06	233.04	218.43	210.22
30000	349.92	313.27	279.64	262.11	252.26
35000	408.24	365.48	326.25	305.80	294.30
40000	466.55	417.69	372.86	349.48	336.35
45000	524.87	469.91	419.46	393.17	378.39
46000	536.54	480.35	428.79	401.91	386.80
47000	548.20	490.79	438.11	410.64	395.21
48000	559.86	501.23	447.43	419.38	403.62
49000	571.53	511.68	456.75	428.12	412.02
50000	583.19	522.12	466.07	436.85	420.43
51000	594.86	532.56	475.39	445.59	428.84
52000	606.52	543.00	484.71	454.33	437.25
53000	618.18	553.44	494.03	463.06	445.66
54000	629.85	563.89	503.36	471.80	454.07
55000	641.51	574.33	512.68	480.54	462.47
56000	653.17	584.77	522.00	489.28	470.88
57000	664.84	595.21	531.32	498.01	479.29
58000	676.50	605.66	540.64	506.75	487.70
59000	688.17	616.10	549.96	515.49	496.11
60000	699.83	626.54	559.28	524.22	504.52
61000	711.49	636.98	568.61	532.96	512.93
62000	723.16	647.42	577.93	541.70	521.33
63000	734.82	657.87	587.25	550.43	529.74
64000	746.48	668.31	596.57	559.17	538.15
65000	758.15	678.75	605.89	567.91	546.56
67500	787.31	704.86	629.19	589.75	567.58
70000	816.47	730.96	652.50	611.59	588.60
75000	874.78	783.17	699.10	655.28	630.65
80000	933.10	835.38	745.71	698.96	672.69
85000	991.42	887.60	792.32	742.65	714.73
90000	1049.74	939.81	838.92	786.33	756.77
95000	1108.06	992.02	885.53	830.02	798.82
100000	1166.38	1044.23	932.14	873.70	840.86
105000	1224.70	1096.44	978.74	917.39	882.90
110000	1283.02	1148.65	1025.35	961.07	924.94
115000	1341.33	1200.86	1071.96	1004.76	966.99
120000	1399.65	1253.07	1118.56	1048.44	1009.03
125000	1457.97	1305.29	1165.17	1092.13	1051.07
130000	1516.29	1357.50	1211.78	1135.81	1093.12
135000	1574.61	1409.71	1258.38	1179.50	1135.16
140000	1632.93	1461.92	1304.99	1223.18	1177.20
145000	1691.25	1514.13	1351.60	1266.87	1219.24
150000	1749.56	1566.34	1398.20	1310.55	1261.29

10%   MONTHLY PAYMENT
necessary to amortize a loan

AMOUNT	1 YEAR	3 YEARS	5 YEARS	8 YEARS	10 YEARS
$ 50	4.40	1.62	1.07	.76	.67
100	8.80	3.23	2.13	1.52	1.33
200	17.59	6.46	4.25	3.04	2.65
300	26.38	9.69	6.38	4.56	3.97
400	35.17	12.91	8.50	6.07	5.29
500	43.96	16.14	10.63	7.59	6.61
600	52.75	19.37	12.75	9.11	7.93
700	61.55	22.59	14.88	10.63	9.26
800	70.34	25.82	17.00	12.14	10.58
900	79.13	29.05	19.13	13.66	11.90
1000	87.92	32.27	21.25	15.18	13.22
2000	175.84	64.54	42.50	30.35	26.44
3000	263.75	96.81	63.75	45.53	39.65
4000	351.67	129.07	84.99	60.70	52.87
5000	439.58	161.34	106.24	75.88	66.08
6000	527.50	193.61	127.49	91.05	79.30
7000	615.42	225.88	148.73	106.22	92.51
8000	703.33	258.14	169.98	121.40	105.73
9000	791.25	290.41	191.23	136.57	118.94
10000	879.16	322.68	212.48	151.75	132.16
15000	1318.74	484.01	318.71	227.62	198.23
20000	1758.32	645.35	424.95	303.49	264.31
25000	2197.90	806.68	531.18	379.36	330.38
30000	2637.48	968.02	637.42	455.23	396.46
35000	3077.06	1129.36	743.65	531.10	462.53
40000	3516.64	1290.69	849.89	606.97	528.61
45000	3956.22	1452.03	956.12	682.84	594.68
46000	4044.14	1484.30	977.37	698.02	607.90
47000	4132.05	1516.56	998.62	713.19	621.11
48000	4219.97	1548.83	1019.86	728.36	634.33
49000	4307.88	1581.10	1041.11	743.54	647.54
50000	4395.80	1613.36	1062.36	758.71	660.76
51000	4483.72	1645.63	1083.60	773.89	673.97
52000	4571.63	1677.90	1104.85	789.06	687.19
53000	4659.55	1710.17	1126.10	804.24	700.40
54000	4747.46	1742.43	1147.35	819.41	713.62
55000	4835.38	1774.70	1168.59	834.58	726.83
56000	4923.29	1806.97	1189.84	849.76	740.05
57000	5011.21	1839.23	1211.09	864.93	753.26
58000	5099.13	1871.50	1232.33	880.11	766.48
59000	5187.04	1903.77	1253.58	895.28	779.69
60000	5274.96	1936.04	1274.83	910.45	792.91
61000	5362.87	1968.30	1296.07	925.63	806.12
62000	5450.79	2000.57	1317.32	940.80	819.34
63000	5538.71	2032.84	1338.57	955.98	832.55
64000	5626.62	2065.10	1359.82	971.15	845.77
65000	5714.54	2097.37	1381.06	986.33	858.98
67500	5934.33	2178.04	1434.18	1024.26	892.02
70000	6154.12	2258.71	1487.30	1062.20	925.06
75000	6593.70	2420.04	1593.53	1138.07	991.14
80000	7033.28	2581.38	1699.77	1213.94	1057.21
85000	7472.86	2742.72	1806.00	1289.81	1123.29
90000	7912.43	2904.05	1912.24	1365.68	1189.36
95000	8352.01	3065.39	2018.47	1441.55	1255.44
100000	8791.59	3226.72	2124.71	1517.42	1321.51
105000	9231.17	3388.06	2230.94	1593.29	1387.59
110000	9670.75	3549.40	2337.18	1669.16	1453.66
115000	10110.33	3710.73	2443.42	1745.03	1519.74
120000	10549.91	3872.07	2549.65	1820.90	1585.81
125000	10989.49	4033.40	2655.89	1896.78	1651.89
130000	11429.07	4194.74	2762.12	1972.65	1717.96
135000	11868.65	4356.08	2868.36	2048.52	1784.04
140000	12308.23	4517.41	2974.59	2124.39	1850.12
145000	12747.81	4678.75	3080.83	2200.26	1916.19
150000	13187.39	4840.08	3187.06	2276.13	1982.27

MONTHLY PAYMENT 10%
necessary to amortize a loan

AMOUNT	12 YEARS	15 YEARS	20 YEARS	25 YEARS	30 YEARS
$ 50	.60	.54	.49	.46	.44
100	1.20	1.08	.97	.91	.88
200	2.40	2.15	1.94	1.82	1.76
300	3.59	3.23	2.90	2.73	2.64
400	4.79	4.30	3.87	3.64	3.52
500	5.98	5.38	4.83	4.55	4.39
600	7.18	6.45	5.80	5.46	5.27
700	8.37	7.53	6.76	6.37	6.15
800	9.57	8.60	7.73	7.27	7.03
900	10.76	9.68	8.69	8.18	7.90
1000	11.96	10.75	9.66	9.09	8.78
2000	23.91	21.50	19.31	18.18	17.56
3000	35.86	32.24	28.96	27.27	26.33
4000	47.81	42.99	38.61	36.35	35.11
5000	59.76	53.74	48.26	45.44	43.88
6000	71.71	64.48	57.91	54.53	52.66
7000	83.66	75.23	67.56	63.61	61.44
8000	95.61	85.97	77.21	72.70	70.21
9000	107.56	96.72	86.86	81.79	78.99
10000	119.51	107.47	96.51	90.88	87.76
15000	179.27	161.20	144.76	136.31	131.64
20000	239.02	214.93	193.01	181.75	175.52
25000	298.77	268.66	241.26	227.18	219.40
30000	358.53	322.39	289.51	272.62	263.28
35000	418.28	376.12	337.76	318.05	307.16
40000	478.04	429.85	386.01	363.49	351.03
45000	537.79	483.58	434.26	408.92	394.91
46000	549.74	494.32	443.91	418.01	403.69
47000	561.69	505.07	453.57	427.09	412.46
48000	573.64	515.82	463.22	436.18	421.24
49000	585.59	526.56	472.87	445.27	430.02
50000	597.54	537.31	482.52	454.36	438.79
51000	609.49	548.05	492.17	463.44	447.57
52000	621.45	558.80	501.82	472.53	456.34
53000	633.40	569.55	511.47	481.62	465.12
54000	645.35	580.29	521.12	490.70	473.89
55000	657.30	591.04	530.77	499.79	482.67
56000	669.25	601.78	540.42	508.88	491.45
57000	681.20	612.53	550.07	517.96	500.22
58000	693.15	623.28	559.72	527.05	509.00
59000	705.10	634.02	569.37	536.14	517.77
60000	717.05	644.77	579.02	545.23	526.55
61000	729.00	655.51	588.67	554.31	535.32
62000	740.95	666.26	598.32	563.40	544.10
63000	752.90	677.01	607.97	572.49	552.88
64000	764.86	687.75	617.62	581.57	561.65
65000	776.81	698.50	627.27	590.66	570.43
67500	806.68	725.36	651.39	613.38	592.37
70000	836.56	752.23	675.52	636.10	614.31
75000	896.31	805.96	723.77	681.53	658.18
80000	956.07	859.69	772.02	726.97	702.06
85000	1015.82	913.42	820.27	772.40	745.94
90000	1075.58	967.15	868.52	817.84	789.82
95000	1135.33	1020.88	916.78	863.27	833.70
100000	1195.08	1074.61	965.03	908.71	877.58
105000	1254.84	1128.34	1013.28	954.14	921.46
110000	1314.59	1182.07	1061.53	999.58	965.33
115000	1374.35	1235.80	1109.78	1045.01	1009.21
120000	1434.10	1289.53	1158.03	1090.45	1053.09
125000	1493.85	1343.26	1206.28	1135.88	1096.97
130000	1553.61	1396.99	1254.53	1181.32	1140.85
135000	1613.36	1450.72	1302.78	1226.75	1184.73
140000	1673.11	1504.45	1351.04	1272.19	1228.61
145000	1732.87	1558.18	1399.29	1317.62	1272.48
150000	1792.62	1611.91	1447.54	1363.06	1316.36

10.5%

MONTHLY PAYMENT
necessary to amortize a loan

AMOUNT	1 YEAR	3 YEARS	5 YEARS	8 YEARS	10 YEARS
$ 50	4.41	1.63	1.08	.78	.68
100	8.82	3.26	2.15	1.55	1.35
200	17.63	6.51	4.30	3.09	2.70
300	26.45	9.76	6.45	4.64	4.05
400	35.26	13.01	8.60	6.18	5.40
500	44.08	16.26	10.75	7.73	6.75
600	52.89	19.51	12.90	9.27	8.10
700	61.71	22.76	15.05	10.81	9.45
800	70.52	26.01	17.20	12.36	10.80
900	79.34	29.26	19.35	13.90	12.15
1000	88.15	32.51	21.50	15.45	13.50
2000	176.30	65.01	42.99	30.89	26.99
3000	264.45	97.51	64.49	46.33	40.49
4000	352.60	130.01	85.98	61.77	53.98
5000	440.75	162.52	107.47	77.21	67.47
6000	528.90	195.02	128.97	92.65	80.97
7000	617.05	227.52	150.46	108.09	94.46
8000	705.19	260.02	171.96	123.53	107.95
9000	793.34	292.53	193.45	138.97	121.45
10000	881.49	325.03	214.94	154.41	134.94
15000	1322.23	487.54	322.41	231.61	202.41
20000	1762.98	650.05	429.88	308.81	269.87
25000	2203.72	812.57	537.35	386.01	337.34
30000	2644.46	975.08	644.82	463.21	404.81
35000	3085.21	1137.59	752.29	540.41	472.28
40000	3525.95	1300.10	859.76	617.61	539.74
45000	3966.69	1462.61	967.23	694.81	607.21
46000	4054.84	1495.12	988.72	710.25	620.71
47000	4142.99	1527.62	1010.22	725.69	634.20
48000	4231.14	1560.12	1031.71	741.13	647.69
49000	4319.29	1592.62	1053.21	756.57	661.19
50000	4407.44	1625.13	1074.70	772.01	674.68
51000	4495.58	1657.63	1096.19	787.45	688.17
52000	4583.73	1690.13	1117.69	802.89	701.67
53000	4671.88	1722.63	1139.18	818.33	715.16
54000	4760.03	1755.14	1160.68	833.77	728.65
55000	4848.18	1787.64	1182.17	849.21	742.15
56000	4936.33	1820.14	1203.66	864.65	755.64
57000	5024.48	1852.64	1225.16	880.09	769.13
58000	5112.62	1885.15	1246.65	895.53	782.63
59000	5200.77	1917.65	1268.15	910.97	796.12
60000	5288.92	1950.15	1289.64	926.41	809.61
61000	5377.07	1982.65	1311.13	941.85	823.11
62000	5465.22	2015.16	1332.63	957.29	836.60
63000	5553.37	2047.66	1354.12	972.73	850.10
64000	5641.52	2080.16	1375.61	988.17	863.59
65000	5729.66	2112.66	1397.11	1003.61	877.08
67500	5950.04	2193.92	1450.84	1042.21	910.82
70000	6170.41	2275.18	1504.58	1080.81	944.55
75000	6611.15	2437.69	1612.05	1158.01	1012.02
80000	7051.89	2600.20	1719.52	1235.21	1079.48
85000	7492.64	2762.71	1826.99	1312.41	1146.95
90000	7933.38	2925.22	1934.46	1389.61	1214.42
95000	8374.12	3087.74	2041.93	1466.81	1281.89
100000	8814.87	3250.25	2149.40	1544.01	1349.35
105000	9255.61	3412.76	2256.86	1621.21	1416.82
110000	9696.35	3575.27	2364.33	1698.41	1484.29
115000	10137.09	3737.79	2471.80	1775.61	1551.76
120000	10577.84	3900.30	2579.27	1852.81	1619.22
125000	11018.58	4062.81	2686.74	1930.01	1686.69
130000	11459.32	4225.32	2794.21	2007.21	1754.16
135000	11900.07	4387.83	2901.68	2084.41	1821.63
140000	12340.81	4550.35	3009.15	2161.61	1889.09
145000	12781.55	4712.86	3116.62	2238.81	1956.56
150000	13222.30	4875.37	3224.09	2316.01	2024.03

MONTHLY PAYMENT 10.5%
necessary to amortize a loan

AMOUNT	12 YEARS	15 YEARS	20 YEARS	25 YEARS	30 YEARS
$ 50	.62	.56	.50	.48	.46
100	1.23	1.11	1.00	.95	.92
200	2.45	2.22	2.00	1.89	1.83
300	3.68	3.32	3.00	2.84	2.75
400	4.90	4.43	4.00	3.78	3.66
500	6.13	5.53	5.00	4.73	4.58
600	7.35	6.64	6.00	5.67	5.49
700	8.57	7.74	6.99	6.61	6.41
800	9.80	8.85	7.99	7.56	7.32
900	11.02	9.95	8.99	8.50	8.24
1000	12.25	11.06	9.99	9.45	9.15
2000	24.49	22.11	19.97	18.89	18.30
3000	36.73	33.17	29.96	28.33	27.45
4000	48.97	44.22	39.94	37.77	36.59
5000	61.21	55.27	49.92	47.21	45.74
6000	73.45	66.33	59.91	56.66	54.89
7000	85.69	77.38	69.89	66.10	64.04
8000	97.94	88.44	79.88	75.54	73.18
9000	110.18	99.49	89.86	84.98	82.33
10000	122.42	110.54	99.84	94.42	91.48
15000	183.63	165.81	149.76	141.63	137.22
20000	244.83	221.08	199.68	188.84	182.95
25000	306.04	276.35	249.60	236.05	228.69
30000	367.25	331.62	299.52	283.26	274.43
35000	428.45	386.89	349.44	330.47	320.16
40000	489.66	442.16	399.36	377.68	365.90
45000	550.87	497.43	449.28	424.89	411.64
46000	563.11	508.49	459.26	434.33	420.79
47000	575.35	519.54	469.24	443.77	429.93
48000	587.59	530.60	479.23	453.21	439.08
49000	599.83	541.65	489.21	462.65	448.23
50000	612.08	552.70	499.19	472.10	457.37
51000	624.32	563.76	509.18	481.54	466.52
52000	636.56	574.81	519.16	490.98	475.67
53000	648.80	585.87	529.15	500.42	484.82
54000	661.04	596.92	539.13	509.86	493.96
55000	673.28	607.97	549.11	519.30	503.11
56000	685.52	619.03	559.10	528.75	512.26
57000	697.77	630.08	569.08	538.19	521.41
58000	710.01	641.14	579.07	547.63	530.55
59000	722.25	652.19	589.05	557.07	539.70
60000	734.49	663.24	599.03	566.51	548.85
61000	746.73	674.30	609.02	575.96	558.00
62000	758.97	685.35	619.00	585.40	567.14
63000	771.21	696.41	628.98	594.84	576.29
64000	783.46	707.46	638.97	604.28	585.44
65000	795.70	718.51	648.95	613.72	594.59
67500	826.30	746.15	673.91	637.33	617.45
70000	856.90	773.78	698.87	660.93	640.32
75000	918.11	829.05	748.79	708.14	686.06
80000	979.32	884.32	798.71	755.35	731.80
85000	1040.52	939.59	848.63	802.56	777.53
90000	1101.73	994.86	898.55	849.77	823.27
95000	1162.94	1050.13	948.47	896.98	869.01
100000	1224.15	1105.40	998.38	944.19	914.74
105000	1285.35	1160.67	1048.30	991.40	960.48
110000	1346.56	1215.94	1098.22	1038.60	1006.22
115000	1407.77	1271.21	1148.14	1085.81	1051.96
120000	1468.97	1326.48	1198.06	1133.02	1097.69
125000	1530.18	1381.75	1247.98	1180.23	1143.43
130000	1591.39	1437.02	1297.90	1227.44	1189.17
135000	1652.59	1492.29	1347.82	1274.65	1234.90
140000	1713.80	1547.56	1397.74	1321.86	1280.64
145000	1775.01	1602.83	1447.66	1369.07	1326.38
150000	1836.22	1658.10	1497.57	1416.28	1372.11

11%　　MONTHLY PAYMENT
necessary to amortize a loan

AMOUNT	1 YEAR	3 YEARS	5 YEARS	8 YEARS	10 YEARS
$ 50	4.42	1.64	1.09	.79	.69
100	8.84	3.28	2.18	1.58	1.38
200	17.68	6.55	4.35	3.15	2.76
300	26.52	9.83	6.53	4.72	4.14
400	35.36	13.10	8.70	6.29	5.52
500	44.20	16.37	10.88	7.86	6.89
600	53.03	19.65	13.05	9.43	8.27
700	61.87	22.92	15.22	11.00	9.65
800	70.71	26.20	17.40	12.57	11.03
900	79.55	29.47	19.57	14.14	12.40
1000	88.39	32.74	21.75	15.71	13.78
2000	176.77	65.48	43.49	31.42	27.56
3000	265.15	98.22	65.23	47.13	41.33
4000	353.53	130.96	86.97	62.84	55.11
5000	441.91	163.70	108.72	78.55	68.88
6000	530.29	196.44	130.46	94.26	82.66
7000	618.68	229.18	152.20	109.96	96.43
8000	707.06	261.91	173.94	125.67	110.21
9000	795.44	294.65	195.69	141.38	123.98
10000	883.82	327.39	217.43	157.09	137.76
15000	1325.73	491.09	326.14	235.63	206.63
20000	1767.64	654.78	434.85	314.17	275.51
25000	2209.55	818.47	543.57	392.72	344.38
30000	2651.45	982.17	652.28	471.26	413.26
35000	3093.36	1145.86	760.99	549.80	482.13
40000	3535.27	1309.55	869.70	628.34	551.01
45000	3977.18	1473.25	978.41	706.88	619.88
46000	4065.56	1505.99	1000.16	722.59	633.66
47000	4153.94	1538.72	1021.90	738.30	647.43
48000	4242.32	1571.46	1043.64	754.01	661.21
49000	4330.71	1604.20	1065.38	769.72	674.98
50000	4419.09	1636.94	1087.13	785.43	688.76
51000	4507.47	1669.68	1108.87	801.13	702.53
52000	4595.85	1702.42	1130.61	816.84	716.31
53000	4684.23	1735.16	1152.35	832.55	730.08
54000	4772.61	1767.90	1174.10	848.26	743.86
55000	4861.00	1800.63	1195.84	863.97	757.63
56000	4949.38	1833.37	1217.58	879.68	771.41
57000	5037.76	1866.11	1239.32	895.39	785.18
58000	5126.14	1898.85	1261.07	911.09	798.96
59000	5214.52	1931.59	1282.81	926.80	812.73
60000	5302.90	1964.33	1304.55	942.51	826.51
61000	5391.29	1997.07	1326.29	958.22	840.28
62000	5479.67	2029.81	1348.04	973.93	854.06
63000	5568.05	2062.54	1369.78	989.64	867.83
64000	5656.43	2095.28	1391.52	1005.34	881.61
65000	5744.81	2128.02	1413.26	1021.05	895.38
67500	5965.77	2209.87	1467.62	1060.32	929.82
70000	6186.72	2291.72	1521.97	1099.59	964.26
75000	6628.63	2455.41	1630.69	1178.14	1033.13
80000	7070.54	2619.10	1739.40	1256.68	1102.01
85000	7512.45	2782.80	1848.11	1335.22	1170.88
90000	7954.35	2946.49	1956.82	1413.76	1239.76
95000	8396.26	3110.18	2065.54	1492.31	1308.63
100000	8838.17	3273.88	2174.25	1570.85	1377.51
105000	9280.08	3437.57	2282.96	1649.39	1446.38
110000	9721.99	3601.26	2391.67	1727.93	1515.26
115000	10163.90	3764.96	2500.38	1806.47	1584.13
120000	10605.80	3928.65	2609.10	1885.02	1653.01
125000	11047.71	4092.34	2717.81	1963.56	1721.88
130000	11489.62	4256.04	2826.52	2042.10	1790.76
135000	11931.53	4419.73	2935.23	2120.64	1859.63
140000	12373.44	4583.43	3043.94	2199.18	1928.51
145000	12815.35	4747.12	3152.66	2277.73	1997.38
150000	13257.25	4910.81	3261.37	2356.27	2066.26

MONTHLY PAYMENT   11%
necessary to amortize a loan

AMOUNT	12 YEARS	15 YEARS	20 YEARS	25 YEARS	30 YEARS
$ 50	.63	.57	.52	.50	.48
100	1.26	1.14	1.04	.99	.96
200	2.51	2.28	2.07	1.97	1.91
300	3.77	3.41	3.10	2.95	2.86
400	5.02	4.55	4.13	3.93	3.81
500	6.27	5.69	5.17	4.91	4.77
600	7.53	6.82	6.20	5.89	5.72
700	8.78	7.96	7.23	6.87	6.67
800	10.03	9.10	8.26	7.85	7.62
900	11.29	10.23	9.29	8.83	8.58
1000	12.54	11.37	10.33	9.81	9.53
2000	25.08	22.74	20.65	19.61	19.05
3000	37.61	34.10	30.97	29.41	28.57
4000	50.15	45.47	41.29	39.21	38.10
5000	62.68	56.83	51.61	49.01	47.62
6000	75.22	68.20	61.94	58.81	57.14
7000	87.75	79.57	72.26	68.61	66.67
8000	100.29	90.93	82.58	78.41	76.19
9000	112.82	102.30	92.90	88.22	85.71
10000	125.36	113.66	103.22	98.02	95.24
15000	188.04	170.49	154.83	147.02	142.85
20000	250.72	227.32	206.44	196.03	190.47
25000	313.39	284.15	258.05	245.03	238.09
30000	376.07	340.98	309.66	294.04	285.70
35000	438.75	397.81	361.27	343.04	333.32
40000	501.43	454.64	412.88	392.05	380.93
45000	564.10	511.47	464.49	441.06	428.55
46000	576.64	522.84	474.81	450.86	438.07
47000	589.18	534.21	485.13	460.66	447.60
48000	601.71	545.57	495.46	470.46	457.12
49000	614.25	556.94	505.78	480.26	466.64
50000	626.78	568.30	516.10	490.06	476.17
51000	639.32	579.67	526.42	499.86	485.69
52000	651.85	591.04	536.74	509.66	495.21
53000	664.39	602.40	547.06	519.46	504.74
54000	676.92	613.77	557.39	529.27	514.26
55000	689.46	625.13	567.71	539.07	523.78
56000	702.00	636.50	578.03	548.87	533.31
57000	714.53	647.87	588.35	558.67	542.83
58000	727.07	659.23	598.67	568.47	552.35
59000	739.60	670.60	609.00	578.27	561.88
60000	752.14	681.96	619.32	588.07	571.40
61000	764.67	693.33	629.64	597.87	580.92
62000	777.21	704.70	639.96	607.68	590.45
63000	789.74	716.06	650.28	617.48	599.97
64000	802.28	727.43	660.61	627.28	609.49
65000	814.82	738.79	670.93	637.08	619.02
67500	846.15	767.21	696.73	661.58	642.82
70000	877.49	795.62	722.54	686.08	666.63
75000	940.17	852.45	774.15	735.09	714.25
80000	1002.85	909.28	825.76	784.10	761.86
85000	1065.53	966.11	877.37	833.10	809.48
90000	1128.20	1022.94	928.97	882.11	857.10
95000	1190.88	1079.77	980.58	931.11	904.71
100000	1253.56	1136.60	1032.19	980.12	952.33
105000	1316.24	1193.43	1083.80	1029.12	999.94
110000	1378.92	1250.26	1135.41	1078.13	1047.56
115000	1441.59	1307.09	1187.02	1127.14	1095.18
120000	1504.27	1363.92	1238.63	1176.14	1142.79
125000	1566.95	1420.75	1290.24	1225.15	1190.41
130000	1629.63	1477.58	1341.85	1274.15	1238.03
135000	1692.30	1534.41	1393.46	1323.16	1285.64
140000	1754.98	1591.24	1445.07	1372.16	1333.26
145000	1817.66	1648.07	1496.68	1421.17	1380.87
150000	1880.34	1704.90	1548.29	1470.17	1428.49

11.5% MONTHLY PAYMENT
necessary to amortize a loan

AMOUNT	1 YEAR	3 YEARS	5 YEARS	8 YEARS	10 YEARS
$ 50	4.44	1.65	1.10	.80	.71
100	8.87	3.30	2.20	1.60	1.41
200	17.73	6.60	4.40	3.20	2.82
300	26.59	9.90	6.60	4.80	4.22
400	35.45	13.20	8.80	6.40	5.63
500	44.31	16.49	11.00	7.99	7.03
600	53.17	19.79	13.20	9.59	8.44
700	62.04	23.09	15.40	11.19	9.85
800	70.90	26.39	17.60	12.79	11.25
900	79.76	29.68	19.80	14.39	12.66
1000	88.62	32.98	22.00	15.98	14.06
2000	177.24	65.96	43.99	31.96	28.12
3000	265.85	98.93	65.98	47.94	42.18
4000	354.47	131.91	87.98	63.92	56.24
5000	443.08	164.89	109.97	79.90	70.30
6000	531.70	197.86	131.96	95.88	84.36
7000	620.31	230.84	153.95	111.86	98.42
8000	708.93	263.81	175.95	127.84	112.48
9000	797.54	296.79	197.94	143.82	126.54
10000	886.16	329.77	219.93	159.80	140.60
15000	1329.23	494.65	329.89	239.70	210.90
20000	1772.31	659.53	439.86	319.59	281.20
25000	2215.38	824.41	549.82	399.49	351.49
30000	2658.46	989.29	659.78	479.39	421.79
35000	3101.53	1154.17	769.75	559.28	492.09
40000	3544.61	1319.05	879.71	639.18	562.39
45000	3987.68	1483.93	989.67	719.08	632.68
46000	4076.30	1516.90	1011.66	735.06	646.74
47000	4164.91	1549.88	1033.66	751.04	660.80
48000	4253.53	1582.85	1055.65	767.01	674.86
49000	4342.14	1615.83	1077.64	782.99	688.92
50000	4430.76	1648.81	1099.64	798.97	702.98
51000	4519.37	1681.78	1121.63	814.95	717.04
52000	4607.99	1714.76	1143.62	830.93	731.10
53000	4696.60	1747.73	1165.61	846.91	745.16
54000	4785.22	1780.71	1187.61	862.89	759.22
55000	4873.83	1813.69	1209.60	878.87	773.28
56000	4962.45	1846.66	1231.59	894.85	787.34
57000	5051.06	1879.64	1253.58	910.83	801.40
58000	5139.68	1912.61	1275.58	926.81	815.46
59000	5228.29	1945.59	1297.57	942.79	829.52
60000	5316.91	1978.57	1319.56	958.77	843.58
61000	5405.52	2011.54	1341.55	974.75	857.64
62000	5494.14	2044.52	1363.55	990.73	871.70
63000	5582.75	2077.49	1385.54	1006.71	885.76
64000	5671.37	2110.47	1407.53	1022.68	899.82
65000	5759.98	2143.45	1429.52	1038.66	913.88
67500	5981.52	2225.89	1484.51	1078.61	949.02
70000	6203.06	2308.33	1539.49	1118.56	984.17
75000	6646.13	2473.21	1649.45	1198.46	1054.47
80000	7089.21	2638.09	1759.41	1278.35	1124.77
85000	7532.28	2802.97	1869.38	1358.25	1195.07
90000	7975.36	2967.85	1979.34	1438.15	1265.36
95000	8418.44	3132.73	2089.30	1518.05	1335.66
100000	8861.51	3297.61	2199.27	1597.94	1405.96
105000	9304.59	3462.49	2309.23	1677.84	1476.26
110000	9747.66	3627.37	2419.19	1757.74	1546.55
115000	10190.74	3792.25	2529.15	1837.63	1616.85
120000	10633.81	3957.13	2639.12	1917.53	1687.15
125000	11076.89	4122.01	2749.08	1997.43	1757.45
130000	11519.96	4286.89	2859.04	2077.32	1827.75
135000	11963.04	4451.77	2969.01	2157.22	1898.04
140000	12406.11	4616.65	3078.97	2237.12	1968.34
145000	12849.19	4781.53	3188.93	2317.01	2038.64
150000	13292.26	4946.41	3298.90	2396.91	2108.94

MONTHLY PAYMENT   11.5%
necessary to amortize a loan

AMOUNT	12 YEARS	15 YEARS	20 YEARS	25 YEARS	30 YEARS
$ 50	.65	.59	.54	.51	.50
100	1.29	1.17	1.07	1.02	1.00
200	2.57	2.34	2.14	2.04	1.99
300	3.85	3.51	3.20	3.05	2.98
400	5.14	4.68	4.27	4.07	3.97
500	6.42	5.85	5.34	5.09	4.96
600	7.70	7.01	6.40	6.10	5.95
700	8.99	8.18	7.47	7.12	6.94
800	10.27	9.35	8.54	8.14	7.93
900	11.55	10.52	9.60	9.15	8.92
1000	12.84	11.69	10.67	10.17	9.91
2000	25.67	23.37	21.33	20.33	19.81
3000	38.50	35.05	32.00	30.50	29.71
4000	51.34	46.73	42.66	40.66	39.62
5000	64.17	58.41	53.33	50.83	49.52
6000	77.00	70.10	63.99	60.99	59.42
7000	89.84	81.78	74.66	71.16	69.33
8000	102.67	93.46	85.32	81.32	79.23
9000	115.50	105.14	95.98	91.49	89.13
10000	128.34	116.82	106.65	101.65	99.03
15000	192.50	175.23	159.97	152.48	148.55
20000	256.67	233.64	213.29	203.30	198.06
25000	320.83	292.05	266.61	254.12	247.58
30000	385.00	350.46	319.93	304.95	297.09
35000	449.17	408.87	373.26	355.77	346.61
40000	513.33	467.28	426.58	406.59	396.12
45000	577.50	525.69	479.90	457.42	445.64
46000	590.33	537.37	490.56	467.58	455.54
47000	603.16	549.05	501.23	477.75	465.44
48000	616.00	560.74	511.89	487.91	475.34
49000	628.83	572.42	522.56	498.07	485.25
50000	641.66	584.10	533.22	508.24	495.15
51000	654.50	595.78	543.88	518.40	505.05
52000	667.33	607.46	554.55	528.57	514.96
53000	680.16	619.15	565.21	538.73	524.86
54000	693.00	630.83	575.88	548.90	534.76
55000	705.83	642.51	586.54	559.06	544.67
56000	718.66	654.19	597.21	569.23	554.57
57000	731.50	665.87	607.87	579.39	564.47
58000	744.33	677.56	618.53	589.56	574.37
59000	757.16	689.24	629.20	599.72	584.28
60000	769.99	700.92	639.86	609.89	594.18
61000	782.83	712.60	650.53	620.05	604.08
62000	795.66	724.28	661.19	630.22	613.99
63000	808.49	735.96	671.86	640.38	623.89
64000	821.33	747.65	682.52	650.55	633.79
65000	834.16	759.33	693.18	660.71	643.69
67500	866.24	788.53	719.85	686.12	668.45
70000	898.33	817.74	746.51	711.53	693.21
75000	962.49	876.15	799.83	762.36	742.72
80000	1026.66	934.56	853.15	813.18	792.24
85000	1090.82	992.97	906.47	864.00	841.75
90000	1154.99	1051.38	959.79	914.83	891.27
95000	1219.16	1109.79	1013.11	965.65	940.78
100000	1283.32	1168.19	1066.43	1016.47	990.30
105000	1347.49	1226.60	1119.76	1067.30	1039.81
110000	1411.65	1285.01	1173.08	1118.12	1089.33
115000	1475.82	1343.42	1226.40	1168.94	1138.84
120000	1539.98	1401.83	1279.72	1219.77	1188.35
125000	1604.15	1460.24	1333.04	1270.59	1237.87
130000	1668.32	1518.65	1386.36	1321.41	1287.38
135000	1732.48	1577.06	1439.69	1372.24	1336.90
140000	1796.65	1635.47	1493.01	1423.06	1386.41
145000	1860.81	1693.88	1546.33	1473.88	1435.93
150000	1924.98	1752.29	1599.65	1524.71	1485.44

12% MONTHLY PAYMENT
necessary to amortize a loan

AMOUNT	1 YEAR	3 YEARS	5 YEARS	8 YEARS	10 YEARS
$ 50	4.45	1.67	1.12	.82	.72
100	8.89	3.33	2.23	1.63	1.44
200	17.77	6.65	4.45	3.26	2.87
300	26.66	9.97	6.68	4.88	4.31
400	35.54	13.29	8.90	6.51	5.74
500	44.43	16.61	11.13	8.13	7.18
600	53.31	19.93	13.35	9.76	8.61
700	62.20	23.26	15.58	11.38	10.05
800	71.08	26.58	17.80	13.01	11.48
900	79.97	29.90	20.03	14.63	12.92
1000	88.85	33.22	22.25	16.26	14.35
2000	177.70	66.43	44.49	32.51	28.70
3000	266.55	99.65	66.74	48.76	43.05
4000	355.40	132.86	88.98	65.02	57.39
5000	444.25	166.08	111.23	81.27	71.74
6000	533.10	199.29	133.47	97.52	86.09
7000	621.95	232.51	155.72	113.77	100.43
8000	710.80	265.72	177.96	130.03	114.78
9000	799.64	298.93	200.21	146.28	129.13
10000	888.49	332.15	222.45	162.53	143.48
15000	1332.74	498.22	333.67	243.80	215.21
20000	1776.98	664.29	444.89	325.06	286.95
25000	2221.22	830.36	556.12	406.33	358.68
30000	2665.47	996.43	667.34	487.59	430.42
35000	3109.71	1162.51	778.56	568.85	502.15
40000	3553.96	1328.58	889.78	650.12	573.89
45000	3998.20	1494.65	1001.01	731.38	645.62
46000	4087.05	1527.86	1023.25	747.64	659.97
47000	4175.90	1561.08	1045.49	763.89	674.32
48000	4264.75	1594.29	1067.74	780.14	688.67
49000	4353.60	1627.51	1089.98	796.39	703.01
50000	4442.44	1660.72	1112.23	812.65	717.36
51000	4531.29	1693.93	1134.47	828.90	731.71
52000	4620.14	1727.15	1156.72	845.15	746.05
53000	4708.99	1760.36	1178.96	861.41	760.40
54000	4797.84	1793.58	1201.21	877.66	774.75
55000	4886.69	1826.79	1223.45	893.91	789.10
56000	4975.54	1860.01	1245.69	910.16	803.44
57000	5064.39	1893.22	1267.94	926.42	817.79
58000	5153.23	1926.43	1290.18	942.67	832.14
59000	5242.08	1959.65	1312.43	958.92	846.48
60000	5330.93	1992.86	1334.67	975.18	860.83
61000	5419.78	2026.08	1356.92	991.43	875.18
62000	5508.63	2059.29	1379.16	1007.68	889.52
63000	5597.48	2092.51	1401.41	1023.93	903.87
64000	5686.33	2125.72	1423.65	1040.19	918.22
65000	5775.18	2158.94	1445.89	1056.44	932.57
67500	5997.30	2241.97	1501.51	1097.07	968.43
70000	6219.42	2325.01	1557.12	1137.70	1004.30
75000	6663.66	2491.08	1668.34	1218.97	1076.04
80000	7107.91	2657.15	1779.56	1300.23	1147.77
85000	7552.15	2823.22	1890.78	1381.50	1219.51
90000	7996.40	2989.29	2002.01	1462.76	1291.24
95000	8440.64	3155.36	2113.23	1544.02	1362.98
100000	8884.88	3321.44	2224.45	1625.29	1434.71
105000	9329.13	3487.51	2335.67	1706.55	1506.45
110000	9773.37	3653.58	2446.89	1787.82	1578.19
115000	10217.62	3819.65	2558.12	1869.08	1649.92
120000	10661.86	3985.72	2669.34	1950.35	1721.66
125000	11106.10	4151.79	2780.56	2031.61	1793.39
130000	11550.35	4317.87	2891.78	2112.87	1865.13
135000	11994.59	4483.94	3003.01	2194.14	1936.86
140000	12438.84	4650.01	3114.23	2275.40	2008.60
145000	12883.08	4816.08	3225.45	2356.67	2080.33
150000	13327.32	4982.15	3336.67	2437.93	2152.07

MONTHLY PAYMENT 12%
necessary to amortize a loan

AMOUNT	12 YEARS	15 YEARS	20 YEARS	25 YEARS	30 YEARS
$ 50	.66	.61	.56	.53	.52
100	1.32	1.21	1.11	1.06	1.03
200	2.63	2.41	2.21	2.11	2.06
300	3.95	3.61	3.31	3.16	3.09
400	5.26	4.81	4.41	4.22	4.12
500	6.57	6.01	5.51	5.27	5.15
600	7.89	7.21	6.61	6.32	6.18
700	9.20	8.41	7.71	7.38	7.21
800	10.51	9.61	8.81	8.43	8.23
900	11.83	10.81	9.91	9.48	9.26
1000	13.14	12.01	11.02	10.54	10.29
2000	26.27	24.01	22.03	21.07	20.58
3000	39.41	36.01	33.04	31.60	30.86
4000	52.54	48.01	44.05	42.13	41.15
5000	65.68	60.01	55.06	52.67	51.44
6000	78.81	72.02	66.07	63.20	61.72
7000	91.94	84.02	77.08	73.73	72.01
8000	105.08	96.02	88.09	84.26	82.29
9000	118.21	108.02	99.10	94.80	92.58
10000	131.35	120.02	110.11	105.33	102.87
15000	197.02	180.03	165.17	157.99	154.30
20000	262.69	240.04	220.22	210.65	205.73
25000	328.36	300.05	275.28	263.31	257.16
30000	394.03	360.06	330.33	315.97	308.59
35000	459.70	420.06	385.39	368.63	360.02
40000	525.37	480.07	440.44	421.29	411.45
45000	591.04	540.08	495.49	473.96	462.88
46000	604.18	552.08	506.50	484.49	473.17
47000	617.31	564.08	517.52	495.02	483.45
48000	630.45	576.09	528.53	505.55	493.74
49000	643.58	588.09	539.54	516.08	504.03
50000	656.71	600.09	550.55	526.62	514.31
51000	669.85	612.09	561.56	537.15	524.60
52000	682.98	624.09	572.57	547.68	534.88
53000	696.12	636.09	583.58	558.21	545.17
54000	709.25	648.10	594.59	568.75	555.46
55000	722.39	660.10	605.60	579.28	565.74
56000	735.52	672.10	616.61	589.81	576.03
57000	748.65	684.10	627.62	600.34	586.31
58000	761.79	696.10	638.63	610.88	596.60
59000	774.92	708.10	649.65	621.41	606.89
60000	788.06	720.11	660.66	631.94	617.17
61000	801.19	732.11	671.67	642.47	627.46
62000	814.32	744.11	682.68	653.00	637.74
63000	827.46	756.11	693.69	663.54	648.03
64000	840.59	768.11	704.70	674.07	658.32
65000	853.73	780.11	715.71	684.60	668.60
67500	886.56	810.12	743.24	710.93	694.32
70000	919.40	840.12	770.77	737.26	720.03
75000	985.07	900.13	825.82	789.92	771.46
80000	1050.74	960.14	880.87	842.58	822.90
85000	1116.41	1020.15	935.93	895.25	874.33
90000	1182.08	1080.16	990.98	947.91	925.76
95000	1247.75	1140.16	1046.04	1000.57	977.19
100000	1313.42	1200.17	1101.09	1053.23	1028.62
105000	1379.10	1260.18	1156.15	1105.89	1080.05
110000	1444.77	1320.19	1211.20	1158.55	1131.48
115000	1510.44	1380.20	1266.25	1211.21	1182.91
120000	1576.11	1440.21	1321.31	1263.87	1234.34
125000	1641.78	1500.22	1376.36	1316.54	1285.77
130000	1707.45	1560.22	1431.42	1369.20	1337.20
135000	1773.12	1620.23	1486.47	1421.86	1388.63
140000	1838.79	1680.24	1541.53	1474.52	1440.06
145000	1904.46	1740.25	1596.58	1527.18	1491.49
150000	1970.13	1800.26	1651.63	1579.84	1542.92

12.5% MONTHLY PAYMENT
necessary to amortize a loan

AMOUNT	1 YEAR	3 YEARS	5 YEARS	8 YEARS	10 YEARS
$ 50	4.46	1.68	1.13	.83	.74
100	8.91	3.35	2.25	1.66	1.47
200	17.82	6.70	4.50	3.31	2.93
300	26.73	10.04	6.75	4.96	4.40
400	35.64	13.39	9.00	6.62	5.86
500	44.55	16.73	11.25	8.27	7.32
600	53.45	20.08	13.50	9.92	8.79
700	62.36	23.42	15.75	11.58	10.25
800	71.27	26.77	18.00	13.23	11.72
900	80.18	30.11	20.25	14.88	13.18
1000	89.09	33.46	22.50	16.53	14.64
2000	178.17	66.91	45.00	33.06	29.28
3000	267.25	100.37	67.50	49.59	43.92
4000	356.34	133.82	90.00	66.12	58.56
5000	445.42	167.27	112.49	82.65	73.19
6000	534.50	200.73	134.99	99.18	87.83
7000	623.59	234.18	157.49	115.71	102.47
8000	712.67	267.63	179.99	132.24	117.11
9000	801.75	301.09	202.49	148.76	131.74
10000	890.83	334.54	224.98	165.29	146.38
15000	1336.25	501.81	337.47	247.94	219.57
20000	1781.66	669.08	449.96	330.58	292.76
25000	2227.08	836.35	562.45	413.23	365.95
30000	2672.49	1003.61	674.94	495.87	439.13
35000	3117.91	1170.88	787.43	578.51	512.32
40000	3563.32	1338.15	899.92	661.16	585.51
45000	4008.73	1505.42	1012.41	743.80	658.70
46000	4097.82	1538.87	1034.91	760.33	673.34
47000	4186.90	1572.33	1057.41	776.86	687.97
48000	4275.98	1605.78	1079.91	793.39	702.61
49000	4365.07	1639.23	1102.40	809.92	717.25
50000	4454.15	1672.69	1124.90	826.45	731.89
51000	4543.23	1706.14	1147.40	842.97	746.52
52000	4632.31	1739.59	1169.90	859.50	761.16
53000	4721.40	1773.05	1192.40	876.03	775.80
54000	4810.48	1806.50	1214.89	892.56	790.44
55000	4899.56	1839.95	1237.39	909.09	805.07
56000	4988.65	1873.41	1259.89	925.62	819.71
57000	5077.73	1906.86	1282.39	942.15	834.35
58000	5166.81	1940.32	1304.89	958.68	848.99
59000	5255.89	1973.77	1327.38	975.20	863.62
60000	5344.98	2007.22	1349.88	991.73	878.26
61000	5434.06	2040.68	1372.38	1008.26	892.90
62000	5523.14	2074.13	1394.88	1024.79	907.54
63000	5612.23	2107.58	1417.38	1041.32	922.17
64000	5701.31	2141.04	1439.87	1057.85	936.81
65000	5790.39	2174.49	1462.37	1074.38	951.45
67500	6013.10	2258.12	1518.62	1115.70	988.04
70000	6235.81	2341.76	1574.86	1157.02	1024.64
75000	6681.22	2509.03	1687.35	1239.67	1097.83
80000	7126.63	2676.30	1799.84	1322.31	1171.01
85000	7572.05	2843.56	1912.33	1404.95	1244.20
90000	8017.46	3010.83	2024.82	1487.60	1317.39
95000	8462.88	3178.10	2137.31	1570.24	1390.58
100000	8908.29	3345.37	2249.80	1652.89	1463.77
105000	9353.71	3512.64	2362.29	1735.53	1536.95
110000	9799.12	3679.90	2474.78	1818.17	1610.14
115000	10244.53	3847.17	2587.27	1900.82	1683.33
120000	10689.95	4014.44	2699.76	1983.46	1756.52
125000	11135.36	4181.71	2812.25	2066.11	1829.71
130000	11580.78	4348.98	2924.74	2148.75	1902.90
135000	12026.19	4516.24	3037.23	2231.39	1976.08
140000	12471.61	4683.51	3149.72	2314.04	2049.27
145000	12917.02	4850.78	3262.21	2396.68	2122.46
150000	13362.43	5018.05	3374.70	2479.33	2195.65

MONTHLY PAYMENT
necessary to amortize a loan
12.5%

AMOUNT	12 YEARS	15 YEARS	20 YEARS	25 YEARS	30 YEARS
$ 50	.68	.62	.57	.55	.54
100	1.35	1.24	1.14	1.10	1.07
200	2.69	2.47	2.28	2.19	2.14
300	4.04	3.70	3.41	3.28	3.21
400	5.38	4.94	4.55	4.37	4.27
500	6.72	6.17	5.69	5.46	5.34
600	8.07	7.40	6.82	6.55	6.41
700	9.41	8.63	7.96	7.64	7.48
800	10.76	9.87	9.09	8.73	8.54
900	12.10	11.10	10.23	9.82	9.61
1000	13.44	12.33	11.37	10.91	10.68
2000	26.88	24.66	22.73	21.81	21.35
3000	40.32	36.98	34.09	32.72	32.02
4000	53.76	49.31	45.45	43.62	42.70
5000	67.20	61.63	56.81	54.52	53.37
6000	80.64	73.96	68.17	65.43	64.04
7000	94.08	86.28	79.53	76.33	74.71
8000	107.51	98.61	90.90	87.23	85.39
9000	120.95	110.93	102.26	98.14	96.06
10000	134.39	123.26	113.62	109.04	106.73
15000	201.58	184.88	170.43	163.56	160.09
20000	268.78	246.51	227.23	218.08	213.46
25000	335.97	308.14	284.04	272.59	266.82
30000	403.16	369.76	340.85	327.11	320.18
35000	470.36	431.39	397.65	381.63	373.55
40000	537.55	493.01	454.46	436.15	426.91
45000	604.74	554.64	511.27	490.66	480.27
46000	618.18	566.97	522.63	501.57	490.94
47000	631.62	579.29	533.99	512.47	501.62
48000	645.06	591.62	545.35	523.37	512.29
49000	658.50	603.94	556.71	534.28	522.96
50000	671.93	616.27	568.08	545.18	533.63
51000	685.37	628.59	579.44	556.09	544.31
52000	698.81	640.92	590.80	566.99	554.98
53000	712.25	653.24	602.16	577.89	565.65
54000	725.69	665.57	613.52	588.80	576.32
55000	739.13	677.89	624.88	599.70	587.00
56000	752.57	690.22	636.24	610.60	597.67
57000	766.00	702.54	647.61	621.51	608.34
58000	779.44	714.87	658.97	632.41	619.01
59000	792.88	727.19	670.33	643.31	629.69
60000	806.32	739.52	681.69	654.22	640.36
61000	819.76	751.84	693.05	665.12	651.03
62000	833.20	764.17	704.41	676.02	661.70
63000	846.64	776.49	715.77	686.93	672.38
64000	860.07	788.82	727.13	697.83	683.05
65000	873.51	801.14	738.50	708.74	693.72
67500	907.11	831.96	766.90	735.99	720.40
70000	940.71	862.77	795.30	763.25	747.09
75000	1007.90	924.40	852.11	817.77	800.45
80000	1075.09	986.02	908.92	872.29	853.81
85000	1142.28	1047.65	965.72	926.81	907.17
90000	1209.48	1109.27	1022.53	981.32	960.54
95000	1276.67	1170.90	1079.34	1035.84	1013.90
100000	1343.86	1232.53	1136.15	1090.36	1067.26
105000	1411.06	1294.15	1192.95	1144.88	1120.63
110000	1478.25	1355.78	1249.76	1199.39	1173.99
115000	1545.44	1417.41	1306.57	1253.91	1227.35
120000	1612.63	1479.03	1363.37	1308.43	1280.71
125000	1679.83	1540.66	1420.18	1362.95	1334.08
130000	1747.02	1602.28	1476.99	1417.47	1387.44
135000	1814.21	1663.91	1533.79	1471.98	1440.80
140000	1881.41	1725.54	1590.60	1526.50	1494.17
145000	1948.60	1787.16	1647.41	1581.02	1547.53
150000	2015.79	1848.79	1704.22	1635.54	1600.89

13%   MONTHLY PAYMENT
necessary to amortize a loan

AMOUNT	1 YEAR	3 YEARS	5 YEARS	8 YEARS	10 YEARS
$ 50	4.47	1.69	1.14	.85	.75
100	8.94	3.37	2.28	1.69	1.50
200	17.87	6.74	4.56	3.37	2.99
300	26.80	10.11	6.83	5.05	4.48
400	35.73	13.48	9.11	6.73	5.98
500	44.66	16.85	11.38	8.41	7.47
600	53.60	20.22	13.66	10.09	8.96
700	62.53	23.59	15.93	11.77	10.46
800	71.46	26.96	18.21	13.45	11.95
900	80.39	30.33	20.48	15.13	13.44
1000	89.32	33.70	22.76	16.81	14.94
2000	178.64	67.39	45.51	33.62	29.87
3000	269.96	101.09	68.26	50.43	44.80
4000	357.27	134.78	91.02	67.23	59.73
5000	446.59	168.47	113.77	84.04	74.66
6000	535.91	202.17	136.52	100.85	89.59
7000	625.23	235.86	159.28	117.66	104.52
8000	714.54	269.56	182.03	134.46	119.45
9000	803.86	303.25	204.78	151.27	134.38
10000	893.18	336.94	227.54	168.08	149.32
15000	1339.76	505.41	341.30	252.11	223.97
20000	1786.35	673.88	455.07	336.15	298.63
25000	2232.94	842.35	568.83	420.19	373.28
30000	2679.52	1010.82	682.60	504.22	447.94
35000	3126.11	1179.29	796.36	588.26	522.59
40000	3572.70	1347.76	910.13	672.30	597.25
45000	4019.28	1516.23	1023.89	756.33	671.90
46000	4108.60	1549.93	1046.65	773.14	686.83
47000	4197.92	1583.62	1069.40	789.95	701.77
48000	4287.23	1617.31	1092.15	806.75	716.70
49000	4376.55	1651.01	1114.91	823.56	731.63
50000	4465.87	1684.70	1137.66	840.37	746.56
51000	4555.19	1718.40	1160.41	857.18	761.49
52000	4644.50	1752.09	1183.16	873.98	776.42
53000	4733.82	1785.78	1205.92	890.79	791.35
54000	4823.14	1819.48	1228.67	907.60	806.28
55000	4912.46	1853.17	1251.42	924.40	821.21
56000	5001.77	1886.87	1274.18	941.21	836.15
57000	5091.09	1920.56	1296.93	958.02	851.08
58000	5180.41	1954.25	1319.68	974.83	866.01
59000	5269.72	1987.95	1342.44	991.63	880.94
60000	5359.04	2021.64	1365.19	1008.44	895.87
61000	5448.36	2055.34	1387.94	1025.25	910.80
62000	5537.68	2089.03	1410.70	1042.05	925.73
63000	5626.99	2122.72	1433.45	1058.86	940.66
64000	5716.31	2156.42	1456.20	1075.67	955.59
65000	5805.63	2190.11	1478.95	1092.48	970.52
67500	6028.92	2274.35	1535.84	1134.49	1007.85
70000	6252.21	2358.58	1592.72	1176.51	1045.18
75000	6698.80	2527.05	1706.49	1260.55	1119.84
80000	7145.39	2695.52	1820.25	1344.59	1194.49
85000	7591.97	2863.99	1934.02	1428.62	1269.15
90000	8038.56	3032.46	2047.78	1512.66	1343.80
95000	8485.15	3200.93	2161.55	1596.69	1418.46
100000	8931.73	3369.40	2275.31	1680.73	1493.11
105000	9378.32	3537.87	2389.08	1764.77	1567.77
110000	9824.91	3706.34	2502.84	1848.80	1642.42
115000	10271.49	3874.81	2616.61	1932.84	1717.08
120000	10718.08	4043.28	2730.37	2016.88	1791.73
125000	11164.66	4211.75	2844.14	2100.91	1866.39
130000	11611.25	4380.22	2957.90	2184.95	1941.04
135000	12057.84	4548.69	3071.67	2268.98	2015.70
140000	12504.42	4717.16	3185.44	2353.02	2090.36
145000	12951.01	4885.63	3299.20	2437.06	2165.01
150000	13397.60	5054.10	3412.97	2521.09	2239.67

MONTHLY PAYMENT 13%
necessary to amortize a loan

AMOUNT	12 YEARS	15 YEARS	20 YEARS	25 YEARS	30 YEARS
$ 50	.69	.64	.59	.57	.56
100	1.38	1.27	1.18	1.13	1.11
200	2.75	2.54	2.35	2.26	2.22
300	4.13	3.80	3.52	3.39	3.32
400	5.50	5.07	4.69	4.52	4.43
500	6.88	6.33	5.86	5.64	5.54
600	8.25	7.60	7.03	6.77	6.64
700	9.63	8.86	8.21	7.90	7.75
800	11.00	10.13	9.38	9.03	8.85
900	12.38	11.39	10.55	10.16	9.96
1000	13.75	12.66	11.72	11.28	11.07
2000	27.50	25.31	23.44	22.56	22.13
3000	41.24	37.96	35.15	33.84	33.19
4000	54.99	50.61	46.87	45.12	44.25
5000	68.74	63.27	58.58	56.40	55.31
6000	82.48	75.92	70.30	67.68	66.38
7000	96.23	88.57	82.02	78.95	77.44
8000	109.98	101.22	93.73	90.23	88.50
9000	123.72	113.88	105.45	101.51	99.56
10000	137.47	126.53	117.16	112.79	110.62
15000	206.20	189.79	175.74	169.18	165.93
20000	274.93	253.05	234.32	225.57	221.24
25000	343.66	316.32	292.90	281.96	276.55
30000	412.39	379.58	351.48	338.36	331.86
35000	481.12	442.84	410.06	394.75	387.17
40000	549.86	506.10	468.64	451.14	442.48
45000	618.59	569.36	527.21	507.53	497.79
46000	632.33	582.02	538.93	518.81	508.86
47000	646.08	594.67	550.65	530.09	519.92
48000	659.83	607.32	562.36	541.37	530.98
49000	673.57	619.97	574.08	552.64	542.04
50000	687.32	632.63	585.79	563.92	553.10
51000	701.06	645.28	597.51	575.20	564.17
52000	714.81	657.93	609.22	586.48	575.23
53000	728.56	670.58	620.94	597.76	586.29
54000	742.30	683.24	632.66	609.04	597.35
55000	756.05	695.89	644.37	620.31	608.41
56000	769.80	708.54	656.09	631.59	619.48
57000	783.54	721.19	667.80	642.87	630.54
58000	797.29	733.85	679.52	654.15	641.60
59000	811.03	746.50	691.23	665.43	652.66
60000	824.78	759.15	702.95	676.71	663.72
61000	838.53	771.80	714.67	687.98	674.79
62000	852.27	784.46	726.38	699.26	685.85
63000	866.02	797.11	738.10	710.54	696.91
64000	879.77	809.76	749.81	721.82	707.97
65000	893.51	822.41	761.53	733.10	719.03
67500	927.88	854.04	790.82	761.29	746.69
70000	962.24	885.67	820.11	789.49	774.34
75000	1030.97	948.94	878.69	845.88	829.65
80000	1099.71	1012.20	937.27	902.27	884.96
85000	1168.44	1075.46	995.84	958.67	940.27
90000	1237.17	1138.72	1054.42	1015.06	995.58
95000	1305.90	1201.99	1113.00	1071.45	1050.89
100000	1374.63	1265.25	1171.58	1127.84	1106.20
105000	1443.36	1328.51	1230.16	1184.23	1161.51
110000	1512.09	1391.77	1288.74	1240.62	1216.82
115000	1580.82	1455.03	1347.32	1297.02	1272.13
120000	1649.56	1518.30	1405.90	1353.41	1327.44
125000	1718.29	1581.56	1464.47	1409.80	1382.75
130000	1787.02	1644.82	1523.05	1466.19	1438.06
135000	1855.75	1708.08	1581.63	1522.58	1493.37
140000	1924.48	1771.34	1640.21	1578.97	1548.68
145000	1993.21	1834.61	1698.79	1635.37	1603.99
150000	2061.94	1897.87	1757.37	1691.76	1659.30

13.5% MONTHLY PAYMENT
necessary to amortize a loan

AMOUNT	1 YEAR	3 YEARS	5 YEARS	8 YEARS	10 YEARS
$ 50	4.48	1.70	1.16	.86	.77
100	8.96	3.40	2.31	1.71	1.53
200	17.92	6.79	4.61	3.42	3.05
300	26.87	10.19	6.91	5.13	4.57
400	35.83	13.58	9.21	6.84	6.10
500	44.78	16.97	11.51	8.55	7.62
600	53.74	20.37	13.81	10.26	9.14
700	62.69	23.76	16.11	11.97	10.66
800	71.65	27.15	18.41	13.68	12.19
900	80.60	30.55	20.71	15.38	13.71
1000	89.56	33.94	23.01	17.09	15.23
2000	179.11	67.88	46.02	34.18	30.46
3000	268.66	101.81	69.03	51.27	45.69
4000	358.21	135.75	92.04	68.36	60.91
5000	447.77	169.68	115.05	85.45	76.14
6000	537.32	203.62	138.06	102.53	91.37
7000	626.87	237.55	161.07	119.62	106.60
8000	716.42	271.49	184.08	136.71	121.82
9000	805.97	305.42	207.09	153.80	137.05
10000	895.53	339.36	230.10	170.89	152.28
15000	1343.29	509.03	345.15	256.33	228.42
20000	1791.05	678.71	460.20	341.77	304.55
25000	2238.81	848.39	575.25	427.21	380.69
30000	2686.57	1018.06	690.30	512.65	456.83
35000	3134.33	1187.74	805.35	598.09	532.97
40000	3582.09	1357.42	920.40	683.53	609.10
45000	4029.85	1527.09	1035.45	768.97	685.24
46000	4119.40	1561.03	1058.46	786.06	700.47
47000	4208.95	1594.96	1081.47	803.15	715.69
48000	4298.50	1628.90	1104.48	820.24	730.92
49000	4388.05	1662.83	1127.49	837.32	746.15
50000	4477.61	1696.77	1150.50	854.41	761.38
51000	4567.16	1730.70	1173.51	871.50	776.60
52000	4656.71	1764.64	1196.52	888.59	791.83
53000	4746.26	1798.58	1219.53	905.68	807.06
54000	4835.81	1832.51	1242.54	922.77	822.29
55000	4925.37	1866.45	1265.55	939.85	837.51
56000	5014.92	1900.38	1288.56	956.94	852.74
57000	5104.47	1934.32	1311.57	974.03	867.97
58000	5194.02	1968.25	1334.58	991.12	883.20
59000	5283.57	2002.19	1357.59	1008.21	898.42
60000	5373.13	2036.12	1380.60	1025.29	913.65
61000	5462.68	2070.06	1403.61	1042.38	928.88
62000	5552.23	2103.99	1426.62	1059.47	944.11
63000	5641.78	2137.93	1449.63	1076.56	959.33
64000	5731.33	2171.86	1472.64	1093.65	974.56
65000	5820.89	2205.80	1495.64	1110.74	989.79
67500	6044.77	2290.64	1553.17	1153.46	1027.86
70000	6268.65	2375.48	1610.69	1196.18	1065.93
75000	6716.41	2545.15	1725.74	1281.62	1142.06
80000	7164.17	2714.83	1840.79	1367.06	1218.20
85000	7611.93	2884.50	1955.84	1452.50	1294.34
90000	8059.69	3054.18	2070.89	1537.94	1370.47
95000	8507.45	3223.86	2185.94	1623.38	1446.61
100000	8955.21	3393.53	2300.99	1708.82	1522.75
105000	9402.97	3563.21	2416.04	1794.26	1598.89
110000	9850.73	3732.89	2531.09	1879.70	1675.02
115000	10298.49	3902.56	2646.14	1965.14	1751.16
120000	10746.25	4072.24	2761.19	2050.58	1827.30
125000	11194.01	4241.92	2876.24	2136.02	1903.43
130000	11641.77	4411.59	2991.28	2221.47	1979.57
135000	12089.53	4581.27	3106.33	2306.91	2055.71
140000	12537.29	4750.95	3221.38	2392.35	2131.85
145000	12985.05	4920.62	3336.43	2477.79	2207.98
150000	13432.81	5090.30	3451.48	2563.23	2284.12

MONTHLY PAYMENT 13.5%
necessary to amortize a loan

AMOUNT	12 YEARS	15 YEARS	20 YEARS	25 YEARS	30 YEARS
$ 50	.71	.65	.61	.59	.58
100	1.41	1.30	1.21	1.17	1.15
200	2.82	2.60	2.42	2.34	2.30
300	4.22	3.90	3.63	3.50	3.44
400	5.63	5.20	4.83	4.67	4.59
500	7.03	6.50	6.04	5.83	5.73
600	8.44	7.79	7.25	7.00	6.88
700	9.85	9.09	8.46	8.16	8.02
800	11.25	10.39	9.66	9.33	9.17
900	12.66	11.69	10.87	10.50	10.31
1000	14.06	12.99	12.08	11.66	11.46
2000	28.12	25.97	24.15	23.32	22.91
3000	42.18	38.95	36.23	34.97	34.37
4000	56.23	51.94	48.30	46.63	45.82
5000	70.29	64.92	60.37	58.29	57.28
6000	84.35	77.90	72.45	69.94	68.73
7000	98.41	90.89	84.52	81.60	80.18
8000	112.46	103.87	96.59	93.26	91.64
9000	126.52	116.85	108.67	104.91	103.09
10000	140.58	129.84	120.74	116.57	114.55
15000	210.86	194.75	181.11	174.85	171.82
20000	281.15	259.67	241.48	233.13	229.09
25000	351.43	324.58	301.85	291.42	286.36
30000	421.72	389.50	362.22	349.70	343.63
35000	492.01	454.42	422.59	407.98	400.90
40000	562.29	519.33	482.95	466.26	458.17
45000	632.58	584.25	543.32	524.55	515.44
46000	646.63	597.23	555.40	536.20	526.89
47000	660.69	610.21	567.47	547.86	538.35
48000	674.75	623.20	579.54	559.51	549.80
49000	688.81	636.18	591.62	571.17	561.26
50000	702.86	649.16	603.69	582.83	572.71
51000	716.92	662.15	615.77	594.48	584.17
52000	730.98	675.13	627.84	606.14	595.62
53000	745.04	688.11	639.91	617.80	607.07
54000	759.09	701.10	651.99	629.45	618.53
55000	773.15	714.08	664.06	641.11	629.98
56000	787.21	727.06	676.13	652.77	641.44
57000	801.26	740.05	688.21	664.42	652.89
58000	815.32	753.03	700.28	676.08	664.34
59000	829.38	766.01	712.36	687.74	675.80
60000	843.44	779.00	724.43	699.39	687.25
61000	857.49	791.98	736.50	711.05	698.71
62000	871.55	804.96	748.58	722.70	710.16
63000	885.61	817.95	760.65	734.36	721.61
64000	899.66	830.93	772.72	746.02	733.07
65000	913.72	843.91	784.80	757.67	744.52
67500	948.86	876.37	814.98	786.82	773.16
70000	984.01	908.83	845.17	815.96	801.79
75000	1054.29	973.74	905.54	874.24	859.06
80000	1124.58	1038.66	965.90	932.52	916.33
85000	1194.86	1103.58	1026.27	990.80	973.61
90000	1265.15	1168.49	1086.64	1049.09	1030.88
95000	1335.44	1233.41	1147.01	1107.37	1088.15
100000	1405.72	1298.32	1207.38	1165.65	1145.42
105000	1476.01	1363.24	1267.75	1223.93	1202.69
110000	1546.29	1428.16	1328.12	1282.21	1259.96
115000	1616.58	1493.07	1388.49	1340.50	1317.23
120000	1686.87	1557.99	1448.85	1398.78	1374.50
125000	1757.15	1622.90	1509.22	1457.06	1431.77
130000	1827.44	1687.82	1569.59	1515.34	1489.04
135000	1897.72	1752.74	1629.96	1573.63	1546.31
140000	1968.01	1817.65	1690.33	1631.91	1603.58
145000	2038.29	1882.57	1750.70	1690.19	1660.85
150000	2108.58	1947.48	1811.07	1748.47	1718.12

14% MONTHLY PAYMENT
necessary to amortize a loan

AMOUNT	1 YEAR	3 YEARS	5 YEARS	8 YEARS	10 YEARS
$ 50	4.49	1.71	1.17	.87	.78
100	8.98	3.42	2.33	1.74	1.56
200	17.96	6.84	4.66	3.48	3.11
300	26.94	10.26	6.99	5.22	4.66
400	35.92	13.68	9.31	6.95	6.22
500	44.90	17.09	11.64	8.69	7.77
600	53.88	20.51	13.97	10.43	9.32
700	62.86	23.93	16.29	12.17	10.87
800	71.83	27.35	18.62	13.90	12.43
900	80.81	30.76	20.95	15.64	13.98
1000	89.79	34.18	23.27	17.38	15.53
2000	179.58	68.36	46.54	34.75	31.06
3000	269.37	102.54	69.81	52.12	46.58
4000	359.15	136.72	93.08	69.49	62.11
5000	448.94	170.89	116.35	86.86	77.64
6000	538.73	205.07	139.61	104.23	93.16
7000	628.51	239.25	162.88	121.61	108.69
8000	718.30	273.43	186.15	138.98	124.22
9000	808.09	307.60	209.42	156.35	139.74
10000	897.88	341.78	232.69	173.72	155.27
15000	1346.81	512.67	349.03	260.58	232.90
20000	1795.75	683.56	465.37	347.44	310.54
25000	2244.68	854.45	581.71	434.29	388.17
30000	2693.62	1025.33	698.05	521.15	465.80
35000	3142.55	1196.22	814.39	608.01	543.44
40000	3591.49	1367.11	930.74	694.87	621.07
45000	4040.43	1538.00	1047.08	781.72	698.70
46000	4130.21	1572.18	1070.34	799.09	714.23
47000	4220.00	1606.35	1093.61	816.47	729.76
48000	4309.79	1640.53	1116.88	833.84	745.28
49000	4399.57	1674.71	1140.15	851.21	760.81
50000	4489.36	1708.89	1163.42	868.58	776.34
51000	4579.15	1743.06	1186.69	885.95	791.86
52000	4668.94	1777.24	1209.95	903.32	807.39
53000	4758.72	1811.42	1233.22	920.69	822.92
54000	4848.51	1845.60	1256.49	938.07	838.44
55000	4938.30	1879.77	1279.76	955.44	853.97
56000	5028.08	1913.95	1303.03	972.81	869.50
57000	5117.87	1948.13	1326.30	990.18	885.02
58000	5207.66	1982.31	1349.56	1007.55	900.55
59000	5297.44	2016.49	1372.83	1024.92	916.08
60000	5387.23	2050.66	1396.10	1042.30	931.60
61000	5477.02	2084.84	1419.37	1059.67	947.13
62000	5566.81	2119.02	1442.64	1077.04	962.66
63000	5656.59	2153.20	1465.90	1094.41	978.18
64000	5746.38	2187.37	1489.17	1111.78	993.71
65000	5836.17	2221.55	1512.44	1129.15	1009.24
67500	6060.64	2307.00	1570.61	1172.58	1048.05
70000	6285.10	2392.44	1628.78	1216.01	1086.87
75000	6734.04	2563.33	1745.12	1302.87	1164.50
80000	7182.97	2734.22	1861.47	1389.73	1242.14
85000	7631.91	2905.10	1977.81	1476.58	1319.77
90000	8080.85	3075.99	2094.15	1563.44	1397.40
95000	8529.78	3246.88	2210.49	1650.30	1475.04
100000	8978.72	3417.77	2326.83	1737.16	1552.67
105000	9427.65	3588.66	2443.17	1824.01	1630.30
110000	9876.59	3759.54	2559.51	1910.87	1707.94
115000	10325.52	3930.43	2675.85	1997.73	1785.57
120000	10774.46	4101.32	2792.20	2084.59	1863.20
125000	11223.39	4272.21	2908.54	2171.44	1940.84
130000	11672.33	4443.10	3024.88	2258.30	2018.47
135000	12121.27	4613.99	3141.22	2345.16	2096.10
140000	12570.20	4784.87	3257.56	2432.02	2173.74
145000	13019.14	4955.76	3373.90	2518.87	2251.37
150000	13468.07	5126.65	3490.24	2605.73	2329.00

MONTHLY PAYMENT 14%
necessary to amortize a loan

AMOUNT	12 YEARS	15 YEARS	20 YEARS	25 YEARS	30 YEARS
$ 50	.72	.67	.63	.61	.60
100	1.44	1.34	1.25	1.21	1.19
200	2.88	2.67	2.49	2.41	2.37
300	4.32	4.00	3.74	3.62	3.56
400	5.75	5.33	4.98	4.82	4.74
500	7.19	6.66	6.22	6.02	5.93
600	8.63	8.00	7.47	7.23	7.11
700	10.06	9.33	8.71	8.43	8.30
800	11.50	10.66	9.95	9.64	9.48
900	12.94	11.99	11.20	10.84	10.67
1000	14.38	13.32	12.44	12.04	11.85
2000	28.75	26.64	24.88	24.08	23.70
3000	43.12	39.96	37.31	36.12	35.55
4000	57.49	53.27	49.75	48.16	47.40
5000	71.86	66.59	62.18	60.19	59.25
6000	86.23	79.91	74.62	72.23	71.10
7000	100.60	93.23	87.05	84.27	82.95
8000	114.98	106.54	99.49	96.31	94.79
9000	129.35	119.86	111.92	108.34	106.64
10000	143.72	133.18	124.36	120.38	118.49
15000	215.57	199.77	186.53	180.57	177.74
20000	287.43	266.35	248.71	240.76	236.98
25000	359.29	332.94	310.89	300.95	296.22
30000	431.14	399.53	373.06	361.13	355.47
35000	503.00	466.11	435.24	421.32	414.71
40000	574.86	532.70	497.41	481.51	473.95
45000	646.71	599.29	559.59	541.70	533.20
46000	661.08	612.61	572.02	553.74	545.05
47000	675.45	625.92	584.46	565.77	556.89
48000	689.83	639.24	596.89	577.81	568.74
49000	704.20	652.56	609.33	589.85	580.59
50000	718.57	665.88	621.77	601.89	592.44
51000	732.94	679.19	634.20	613.92	604.29
52000	747.31	692.51	646.64	625.96	616.14
53000	761.68	705.83	659.07	638.00	627.99
54000	776.05	719.15	671.51	650.04	639.84
55000	790.42	732.46	683.94	662.07	651.68
56000	804.80	745.78	696.38	674.11	663.53
57000	819.17	759.10	708.81	686.15	675.38
58000	833.54	772.42	721.25	698.19	687.23
59000	847.91	785.73	733.68	710.22	699.08
60000	862.28	799.05	746.12	722.26	710.93
61000	876.65	812.37	758.55	734.30	722.78
62000	891.02	825.68	770.99	746.34	734.63
63000	905.40	839.00	783.42	758.37	746.47
64000	919.77	852.32	795.86	770.41	758.32
65000	934.14	865.64	808.29	782.45	770.17
67500	970.07	898.93	839.38	812.54	799.79
70000	1005.99	932.22	870.47	842.64	829.42
75000	1077.85	998.81	932.65	902.83	888.66
80000	1149.71	1065.40	994.82	963.01	947.90
85000	1221.56	1131.99	1057.00	1023.20	1007.15
90000	1293.42	1198.57	1119.17	1083.39	1066.39
95000	1365.28	1265.16	1181.35	1143.58	1125.63
100000	1437.13	1331.75	1243.53	1203.77	1184.88
105000	1508.99	1398.33	1305.70	1263.95	1244.12
110000	1580.84	1464.92	1367.88	1324.14	1303.36
115000	1652.70	1531.51	1430.05	1384.33	1362.61
120000	1724.56	1598.09	1492.23	1444.52	1421.85
125000	1796.41	1664.68	1554.41	1504.71	1481.09
130000	1868.27	1731.27	1616.58	1564.89	1540.34
135000	1940.13	1797.86	1678.76	1625.08	1599.58
140000	2011.98	1864.44	1740.93	1685.27	1658.83
145000	2083.84	1931.03	1803.11	1745.46	1718.07
150000	2155.70	1997.62	1865.29	1805.65	1777.31

LOAN PROGRESS CHART
Unpaid Principal Balance on a $1,000 Loan, 30-Year Term

Interest Rate	Elapsed Term in Years				
	3	4	5	8	10
7.0	967	955	941	895	858
7.5	970	959	946	903	868
8.0	973	962	951	910	877
8.5	975	966	955	917	886
9.0	978	969	959	924	894
9.5	980	971	962	930	902
9.75	981	973	964	933	906
10.0	982	974	966	935	909
10.25	982	975	967	938	913
10.5	983	976	969	941	916
11.0	985	979	972	945	923
11.5	986	981	974	950	929
12.0	988	982	977	954	934
12.5	989	984	979	958	939
13.0	990	986	981	962	944
13.5	991	987	983	965	949
14.0	992	988	984	968	953
14.5	993	990	986	971	957
15.0	993	991	987	973	960
15.5	994	992	988	976	964
16.0	995	992	990	978	967
16.5	995	993	991	980	969
17.0	996	994	992	982	972
17.5	996	995	992	983	974
18.0	997	995	993	985	977

LOAN PROGRESS CHART
Unpaid Principal Balance on a $1,000 Loan, 30-Year Term

Interest Rate	Elapsed Term in Years				
	12	15	18	20	25
7.0	816	740	647	573	336
7.5	827	754	663	589	349
8.0	839	768	678	605	362
8.5	849	781	693	620	375
9.0	859	793	707	635	388
9.5	869	805	721	650	400
9.75	873	811	728	657	407
10.0	878	817	734	664	413
10.25	882	822	741	671	419
10.5	886	828	747	678	426
11.0	894	838	760	691	438
11.5	902	848	772	704	450
12.0	909	857	783	717	462
12.5	915	866	794	729	474
13.0	922	874	805	741	486
13.5	927	882	815	752	498
14.0	933	890	824	763	509
14.5	938	897	834	774	520
15.0	942	903	842	784	532
15.5	947	910	851	793	542
16.0	951	916	859	803	553
16.5	955	921	866	812	563
17.0	958	926	874	820	574
17.5	961	931	880	829	584
18.0	964	936	887	836	593

MONTHLY PERCENT
Divide by 12 to Determine Monthly Payment

Interest Rate	Loan Term in Years			
	5	10	15	20
7.0	23.77	13.94	10.79	9.31
7.5	24.05	14.25	11.13	9.67
8.0	24.34	14.56	11.47	10.04
8.5	24.62	14.88	11.82	10.42
9.0	24.92	15.21	12.18	10.80
9.5	25.21	15.53	12.54	11.19
10.0	25.50	15.86	12.90	11.59
10.5	25.80	16.20	13.27	11.99
11.0	26.10	16.54	13.64	12.39
11.5	26.40	16.88	14.02	12.80
12.0	26.70	17.22	14.41	13.22
12.5	27.00	17.57	14.80	13.64
13.0	27.31	17.92	15.19	14.06
13.5	27.62	18.28	15.58	14.49
14.0	27.93	18.64	15.99	14.93
14.5	28.24	19.00	16.39	15.36
15.0	28.55	19.37	16.80	15.81
15.5	28.87	19.73	17.21	16.25
16.0	29.19	20.11	17.63	16.70
16.5	29.51	20.48	18.05	17.15
17.0	29.83	20.86	18.47	17.61
17.5	30.15	21.24	18.90	18.06
18.0	30.48	21.63	19.33	18.52
18.5	30.80	22.01	19.76	18.99
19.0	31.13	22.41	20.20	19.45

Monthly Mortgage Payment = (Loan Amount x Mortgage %) ÷ 12

MONTHLY PERCENT
Divide by 12 to Determine Monthly Payment

Interest Rate	Loan Term in Years			
	25	30	35	40
7.0	8.49	7.99	7.67	7.46
7.5	8.87	8.40	8.10	7.90
8.0	9.27	8.81	8.53	8.35
8.5	9.67	9.23	8.97	8.80
9.0	10.08	9.66	9.41	9.26
9.5	10.49	10.10	9.86	9.73
10.0	10.91	10.54	10.32	10.19
10.5	11.34	10.98	10.78	10.67
11.0	11.77	11.43	11.25	11.14
11.5	12.20	11.89	11.72	11.62
12.0	12.64	12.35	12.19	12.11
12.5	13.09	12.81	12.67	12.59
13.0	13.54	13.28	13.15	13.08
13.5	13.99	13.75	13.63	13.57
14.0	14.45	14.22	14.11	14.06
14.5	14.91	14.70	14.60	14.55
15.0	15.37	15.18	15.09	15.04
15.5	15.84	15.66	15.58	15.54
16.0	16.31	16.14	16.07	16.03
16.5	16.78	16.63	16.56	16.53
17.0	17.26	17.11	17.05	17.02
17.5	17.74	17.60	17.55	17.52
18.0	18.21	18.09	18.04	18.02
18.5	18.69	18.58	18.54	18.52
19.0	19.18	19.07	19.03	19.02

Monthly Mortgage Payment = (Loan Amount x Mortgage %) ÷ 12

Homestead Publishing Company

4455 Torrance Blvd., Suite 220
Torrance, CA 90503

(800) 247-2940 (USA)
(800) 423-7521 (CA)

****

* When Robert Sterling Clark died in New York, the cost of
* administering his estate was $856,747, the executor was
* paid $2,965,683, and the attorney charged $1,065,530. It
* cost $4,822,430 to "protect" Clark's heirs.
*
* Hyde Stewart, an Ohio postman, died leaving $22,864 and
* no Will. When the estate was settled after twenty five
* months, it had paid out $2,077 in administrator's fees and
* $3,500 in attorney's fees.
*
* "Probate Eats Up Nearly Half of an Estate of $19,425" -
* a front page headline in Missouri newspaper.

****

Can this happen to your estate?

How can you avoid falling into the "probate trap"?

THERE IS A SOLUTION...Read on...

Dear Friend:

Probate has a bad name.

Generations ago, the probate system was conceived as one orderly way of transferring the property of a deceased person to his or her heirs. It was designed to protect the heirs.

Today it has become an ugly, legal nightmare where lawyers, clerks, guardians, administrators, estate appraisers and bonding companies bilk widows and orphans out of their

The Cost of Probate

California's probate fees - set by law- are about average among states. These fees are based on the "gross value of estate" and do not include the cost of extraordinary services, such as appraiser's fees, sale of assets, tax preparation, or litigation.

Assets	Minimum Fees
$ 50,000	$ 3,300
100,000	6,300
150,000	8,300
200,000	10,300
300,000	14,300
500,000	22,300
700,000	30,300
1,000,000	42,300
2,000,000	62,300

inheritance.

All across the nation, greedy lawyers in league with conniving judges and bureaucrats plunder huge chunks - and sometimes all - of an estate.

First, let's see what's wrong with probate, and then let's see how you can avoid probate - so that your family can get to keep the assets that are rightfully theirs.

There are three things wrong with probate.

First, it costs too much.

In most states, probate fees are set by law as a percent of the "gross" estate. Say, you left an estate consisting of your home, an automobile, stocks and bonds, savings and a few other personal possessions worth $200,000. The executor's commission and attorney's fees to probate this estate in California would amount to $10,300. Average fees in other states range from 3.8% in Utah to 1% in Alaska.

Let me show you how high the stakes are: Maryland legislature has been trying for the past seven years to ban percentage fees in probate cases; every year a lobby organized by probate lawyers has been able to defeat the bill.

The second thing wrong with probate is that it takes too long.

On the average, it takes two to five years to settle an estate. For all practical purposes, the estate is frozen during probate while the judges, court officials and attorneys have a field day picking it apart. The beneficiaries, in the meantime, wait, wait...and wait. This is why many lawyers would rather write Wills for $60 and then make a bundle when the Will is probated.

The third abuse of probate is the unwanted publicity it creates.

Everything in probate court is a matter of public record and, unfortunately, there're individuals who go from probate court to probate court compiling lists which are then sold to unscrupulous people who prey on widows and try to separate them from their inheritance.

How Can You Escape From the Vagaries of Probate?

Now that you know why you should avoid probate, let me show you the most effective way of doing it.

The law has provided everyone with a magic key to probate exemption: it's called "inter vivo-trust" or a "Living Trust." With a Living Trust, you can pass on your assets to your spouse or children or other heirs in entirety - without delay, and without the lawyers, administrators, courts, or the appraisers skimming off from the top.

Here's how a Living Trust works. You create the trust by preparing a trust instrument in which you simply identify:

- Assets you're transferring to the trust
- Beneficiary of the trust (your spouse, children or other heirs)
- Trustee (i.e., you) who'll manage the trust

Precisely to help you avoid or reduce the costs and the nightmarish problems of probate, we've put together a HOW TO AVOID PROBATE KIT (1988). The Kit is designed for a layperson to transfer his principal assets to a Living Trust, name himself as trustee, and designate beneficiaries who'll inherit the estate - without the rigors of probate - upon his death.

The Kit contains step-by-step instructions, filled out samples, and all the necessary forms you'll need to establish your Living Trust.

By creating a simple Living Trust document, you'd have freed yourself of the legalized larceny of probate. Simple as that.

Essence of Living Trust: Simplicity, Flexibility and Control

Living Trust is set up by you while you're alive. You name yourself as "trustee" and you maintain full control over your assets just as before. You can do whatever you wish to do with them - manage them, sell them, or give them away. The trust does not become effective till you die or become incapacitated.

The person you would designate as beneficiary of the trust (your husband or wife or children) is called "successor trustee." Upon your death, the successor trustee takes over the estate immediately without going through probate and terminates the trust. It's that simple.

Your trust would be a Revocable Living Trust. You can abolish the trust or alter its terms or change the beneficiaries at any time you wish. It provides you with the maximum amount of flexibility.

More Benefits of Living Trust

Let me point out two more benefits of Living Trusts. First, disgruntled heirs find trusts extremely difficult to contest. When an estate goes to probate, the court freezes its assets for several months and asks anyone to come forward and contest the Will if they please. Someone contesting a will doesn't even need to hire a lawyer. But to contest a trust, a disgruntled heir needs to hire a lawyer and file a civil suit. In the meantime, the trustee is free to distribute the assets to the beneficiaries immediately. Your estate isn't tied up in lengthy litigation.

A Living Trust offers another important benefit. A growing number of older Americans are putting their assets into Living Trusts because they want to avoid being placed under a court-appointed guardian if they become unable to manage their affairs. With a Living Trust, you can specify in advance whom you want to manage your affairs if you ever become incompetent.

How Effective Is the Living Trust?

Let's take a simple example of a savings account. Upon your death, the bank would very likely block the account while the Will is being probated. It will not allow any withdrawal from the account without a court order.

However, with a Living Trust, your beneficiary walks into the bank with the trust instrument and the death certificate - and walks out with the money. No two-to-five year delay. No ten percent in expenses. And no publicity.

What Happens If You Own a Business?

Probate can be particularly harsh on a going business. It almost always deals it a fatal blow. Most businesses simply come to a grinding halt while the dead man's Will is being probated. Your business records become public records - open to competitors and creditors alike.

However, under a Living Trust, the successor trustee can continue to run the business without having to wait for the ponderous machinery of judiciary to grind out an approval. Your business doesn't become everybody's business.

A word about taxes. A Revocable Living Trust has no effect on your taxes. There're no advantages nor are there any disadvantages. As a trustee, you'll continue to report all trust transactions on your own income tax return.

In the final analysis, the greatest advantage of a Living Trust lies in the saving of attorneys' fees, administrator's and executor's commissions and court costs. It's a magical, wonderful formula that allows you to avoid probate.

How To Avoid Probate Kit (1988)

People with high-powered attorneys and financial advisers have always used Living Trusts to escape probate. Attorneys often charge hundreds, even thousands of dollars to set up a Living Trust. Legal fees of $700 to $1,800 to set up a simple trust are very common. All too often, an attorney has his secretary type a few standard forms (similar to the ones you'll find in the Kit) and he then turns around and charges you a whopping fee.

Use of a Living Trust is valid in all fifty states. Normally, you would set up the trust in your present state of residence or domicile. However, if you find it more advantageous to have the trust interpreted under the laws of a different state, the Kit allows you to designate your preference.

HOW TO AVOID PROBATE KIT (1988) contains everything you'll need to establish your Living Trust: Ready-to-use forms, step-by-step instructions, actual examples and explanations of various terms. It shows you how to prepare the trust document, how to implement the trust by transferring title to the property to the trust, and eventually, how your beneficiary can distribute the trust assets to himself or herself and dissolve the trust. All in one handy Kit.

Satisfaction Guaranteed - Or Your Money Back

The regular price of HOW TO AVOID PROBATE KIT (1988) is $79. However, in this Special Introductory Offer, you'll save at least 37%. And you can save even more by ordering the second Kit - for your parents, a relative or friend - for only $10. The Kit is backed by a full money-back guarantee. If for any reason you feel that the Kit isn't for you, simply return it within 90 days for an immediate refund. No questions asked. You risk nothing. Act now while you're thinking about it!

Sincerely,

Jay M. Barry

Jay M. Barry

JMB: sp

P.S. Most people simply do not know that there's a perfectly legal, surprisingly simple way of avoiding probate by setting up a Revocable Living Trust. As a recent article in the Wall Street Journal (Feb. 4, 1987) proclaimed, Revocable Living Trusts are becoming a very popular option in estate planning.

With HOW TO AVOID PROBATE KIT(1988), you, too, can leave your family everything you own and enjoy peace of mind. With our offer of free examination, you risk nothing. for fast service, use our toll-free number.

As I was finishing this, I received a letter from one of our subscribers which I would like to share with you: "I had been planning for a long time to set up an inter vivos trust. I had even begun listing attorneys or legal clinics to query as to how much they would charge. Then I received your mail advertising. I said, 'This may be it.' Now, as I am reading and following your book, I am certain my decision was sound."

> To order HOW TO AVOID PROBATE KIT, send $39.95 plus $2 for postage and handling; for two Kits, send $49.95 plus $3 to: Homestead Publishing Company, 4455 Torrance Boulevard, Suite 220, Torrance, CA., 90503. Or use our toll-free number.